FAITH
IN THE
FACE OF
Fear

Donald Hilliard, Jr.

E ergreen
P R E S S

Faith in the Face of Fear
by Donald Hilliard, Jr.
Copyright ©2002 Donald Hilliard, Jr.

ISBN 1-58169-105-X
For Worldwide Distribution
Printed in the U.S.A.

Evergreen Press
P.O. Box 91011 • Mobile, AL 36691
800-367-8203

Table of Contents

Dedication

This book is dedicated to the
Greater Glory of God,
and to the memory of the innocents
who lost their lives on September 11, 2001,
and those who perished trying to save them.

Preface

People of faith have natural, fundamental questions since the catastrophic events of September 11: Why did this tragedy happen? What is God saying to us? What can we learn? How then shall we live? The answers are hard to come by. But just as God has placed us in this difficult situation, He has also given us leaders to help provide the answers.

Reverend Hilliard is one of those leaders. His words of faith have been a balm to many since the dark moments of September 11, enabling them to cope with those events and, indeed, become strengthened by them. I know because I am one of those who have been touched by Reverend Hilliard's words of wisdom, his words of faith, and his firm belief in the workings of the Almighty. We have prayed together in these and other times of crisis. Bishop Hilliard has been an anchor and an ongoing source of clarity and consolation. The way Reverend Hilliard conducts his own life is exemplary and reaffirms Archibald Macleish's profound insight, "Faith is not taught by arguments. It is taught by lives."

In *Faith in the Face of Fear,* Reverend Hilliard helps bring the events of September 11 into perspective. With a discerning and thoughtful eye, he sees the lessons that we are to cull from those events. He maps out for us the life we should be living, stressing the basics that many of us have forgotten: the importance of being grateful for what we have, for family, friends, and for our faith. Reverend Hilliard teaches us that it is through humility and thankfulness that we can overcome our fears.

I found, in *Faith in the Face of Fear,* the comfort and guidance that I have already experienced in Bishop Hilliard's orations and his personal words to me. Others, too, will find guidance in this wondrous book. They will be reminded of the good of God's deeds, as the Psalmist writes: "For upright is the word of God, and all His deeds are done with faithfulness" (Psalm 33:4).

—*Senator Robert G. Torricelli*

Introduction

"God is not ashamed to be called their God, and He hath prepared for them a city" (Heb. 11:6).

I was running late for a breakfast meeting with my pastoral staff at an area hotel, rushing through the parking deck while concluding a cell phone conversation with my publisher. The morning sun was shining brightly, and the hint of the coming autumn blended nicely with summer's end. It was 8:15 a.m.

After a quick greeting and breakfast, I began to discuss the items on my proposed agenda. We had just returned from a summer recess, and I was anxious to get back on track and move forward. In the middle of our conversation, one of our church members came running through the lobby and abruptly interrupted the meeting. "A plane just hit the World Trade Center, and it is on fire!" We all looked up in amazement and with deep concern. I must confess, however, that the news did not immediately register with me.

What does she mean, "The World Trade Center has been hit by a plane?" I wondered. After a quick prayer from my lips, I continued leading my meeting. Within minutes, all cell phones in the room started ringing. We quickly learned that the other tower of the World Trade Center had just been hit and that the Pentagon was on fire. We were under attack! This registered with me—we were under attack!

At that point, we stopped the meeting and my executive pastor led us in prayer. This prayer was slow, deliberate, and full of deep concern. We dispersed after giving out quick assignments. I immediately left, attempted to phone my eldest daughter in college, drove across town to pick up my youngest daughter, and then headed south on the Turnpike to retrieve my second daughter, both in school.

My executive pastor was driven to the church to manage the staff, many of whom had relatives in New York City that day. The rest of the staff was split between checking on their homes and going to the church.

After several unsuccessful attempts, I was finally able to reach my daughter in college and discovered that her campus had been called together to pray in a nearby field. Upon arriving at my other children's schools, I witnessed many anxious parents scurrying children out of classrooms into cars and down the road. There was confusion and great fear among most.

What in the world was going on? By now, Towers One and Two had crumbled to the ground. We were also to learn that another plane had crashed into a nearby field in Pennsylvania. This could not be! How many were killed? How many were yet alive? This was terrorism, indeed!

At the church, support teams were put in place, and the doors of the church were opened and remained that way for several days. That first day, people came in droves, many crying, falling into their seats, and onto their knees. All were praying! We were all praying for survivors...for those lost...for our nation...for ourselves. This same scenario would take place in thousands of churches across the country and around the world.

This was, indeed, the most horrific demonstration of terrorism America had ever experienced. As we watched our televisions that day, it was as if we were watching a Hollywood movie. It seemed so very surreal. This, however, was not a Hollywood movie...this was real! America was under attack and thousands of lives were lost within an hour. We would never, ever be the same again! The entire nation was in shock and in mourning.

"Lord, help me to hope...help me to cope," I remember praying. How would I navigate the congregation through these turbulent times? People were paying close attention to the words coming across America's pulpits. The Sunday following the crisis, the pews of our church were overflowing during every one of our services! Masses of confused, hurting, and hungry souls asked, "Is there a Word from the Lord?"

Some of the messages delivered during those days were the foundation of this book. It is my sincere hope that it proves to be a source of strength and encouragement to all who read it now and in the years to come. I also hope that it proves to be a tribute to both the memory of the thousands of innocent lives lost, their families, and their loved ones that remain.

I want to offer special thanks to my wife, Phyllis, my daughters, Leah, Charisma, and Destiny, and my nephew, Donald. They continue to be a great source of encouragement and inspiration to me. All of our families and friends have become more important and I am truly grateful for mine.

I offer special thanks to Charles Aniton, Francis Stanton-Martinez, Deacon Cynthia Armour, Charles Robbins, Timothy Davis, Janet Bostic-Evans, Juana Bacchus, and Carla Nicole Bacchus for sharing their stories with us. I also offer special thanks to my executive assistant, Monee McGuire, and Deacon Rose Barker for their editorial assistance with this book.

Finally, special thanks and gratitude to the very fine people of The Cathedral Second Baptist Church, in all three locations, to whom these messages were delivered. A more giving, caring, faithful, and faith-filled people are yet to be found. To God belongs the glory!

"We are troubled on every side, yet not distressed; we are perplexed, but not in despair; persecuted, but not forsaken; cast down, but not destroyed" (II Corinthians 4:8-9).

Prayer

Almighty, Everlasting, Ever-caring, Ever-giving, Ever-loving God:

We pause from the busyness of our lives to remain still during these sacred moments. We remember that YOU are God and God, alone, during these moments when our hearts are too often overwhelmed, and so many souls remain restless.

The hour is filled with anxiety, God, and too many lives are yet gripped by fear. We lovingly confess, today, strong "Faith in the Face of Fear."

Since 9-11, we feel that there is a gapping hole at the "ground zero" of our lives. And yet, we trust You to re-design our lives and to build us stronger and better. Yes, we, indeed, confess that You are the Potter and that we are the clay. We place our lives, unequivocally, into Your loving hands.

Ever-merciful God, who forgives all of our sins and heals all of our diseases, we seek Your face, repent of our sins, and turn from our wicked ways. Too often, we have made gods out of our economic and military might. We have made gods out of things and, for this, we are sorry. You, alone, are our God, and we confess strong "Faith in the Face of Fear!"

You, alone, remain our sure defense. Defend us, Almighty God! Blanket your people with Thy mercy and holy power. Sensitize us to the needs of hurting and broken people everywhere, especially those who have not their daily bread, and those whose hearts are yet raw with grief.

Sweet Jesus, comfort the bereaved with the assurance that "Earth has no sorrow that heaven cannot heal."

Yes! Even if this earthen tabernacle in which we live is dissolved, we do have another building not made with hands, eternal in the heavens. We remember today the thousands of innocents whose lives were lost on September 11, 2001 and we continue to give You thanks for our firefighters, EMTS workers, Port Authority elevator operators, pilots, police, and all who gave themselves that day. Their demonstration of courage, care, and concern, with little thought of their own safety, has been etched in time eternal.

Now, wonderful Counselor, Thou who art the "God of our weary years and the God of our silent tears; the very God who has brought us thus far on our way," we trust You and You alone! Wars, rumors of wars, and terrorism will not kill our faith! Yes, we confess strong "Faith in the Face of Fear!"

"Oh, God, our help in ages past, our hope for years to come, our shelter from the stormy blasts, and our eternal home!" Together, we thank You. We thank You that You are, indeed, Jehovah Jireh, our provider and Jehovah Shalom, our peace.

Thank You for being our guiding light through life's

stormy seas. You remain our light and our salvation. We will not fear, and we will not be afraid. We have faith, great "Faith in the Face of Fear!"

And now, Lord, in these days, where each of us is more aware of our own mortality and the fragility of life, we ask that You would prepare our lives for life eternal. Grant us joy unspeakable, health, peace, and prosperity in this life and prepare our souls for that "blessed hope" where the sun shines forever.

In the words of the aged men and women of my youth...

> When praying days are over, and when the time comes where we go in and come out no longer, when our voice is stilled, our eyes are closed and when I prayed my last prayer and preached my last sermon...may the works I have done, speak for me!

Thank You for a heavenly home and a seat in Your kingdom. Thank You for that home where Job declared that, "there the wicked cease from troubling; and there the weary be at rest" (Job 3:17). Thank You for that place of unceasing joy where we shall live in Thy holy presence forever. Acknowledge, Lord, the sheep of Your own fold, the lambs of Your own redeeming, recipients of Thy great salvation.

May the martyrs greet us and the angels bring us into Thy holy city, Jerusalem, and there we shall be where Jesus is, forever. And we thank You for these things, in Thy holy name.

Amen.

Action Steps in Troubled Times

TAKE SOME TIME TO BE STILL
AND KNOW THAT HE IS GOD...HE DOES CARE.

TAKE SOME TIME TO TALK WITH A FRIEND,
FAMILY MEMBER, NEIGHBOR, OR EVEN A
STRANGER.

TAKE SOME TIME TO GET INVOLVED.
OFFER YOUR TIME AND TALENTS TO HELP
SOMEONE ELSE UNTIL TIMES GET BETTER.

TAKE SOME TIME TO MAKE AMENDS.
SEEK FORGIVENESS FOR TRESPASSES
COMMITTED AND FORGIVE THOSE WHO HAVE
TRESPASSED AGAINST YOU.

TAKE SOME TIME TO PRAY.
ASK GOD FOR STRENGTH, COURAGE AND
CONFIDENCE. WAIT IN HIS PRESENCE...
KNOW HIS VOICE.

TAKE SOME TIME TO COUNT YOUR BLESSINGS.
BE GRACIOUS AND GRATEFUL TO THE GOD
WHO HAS GIVEN MUCH.

PART ONE

FEAR NO MORE

*I sought the Lord, and He heard me, and
delivered me from all my fears.*
(Psalm 34:4)

1

Chapter One

When the Bottom Falls Out

Fear comes in many shapes and sizes. It is what drives the gigantic insurance companies and what keeps psychologists' offices full. It affects all of us from early childhood. Who among us never looked under their childhood bed at night, just to be sure? We buy everything from nightlights to security alarm systems to help us cope with it. We watch horror movies and ride dangerous roller coasters trying to overcome it.

The fear that comes when we lose control of our lives is perhaps the worst fear of all. When an unexpected tragedy occurs in our lives, our fear rating zooms off the charts. When the bottom falls out, how can we feel safe and secure?

Have you ever had the bottom fall out in your life?

Some people were married for years, when all of a sudden, out of nowhere, their mate decides that the thrill is gone and they immediately leave the marriage! The bottom has fallen out for that family. Others faithfully work on a job for many long years, showing up early and leaving late. Then one day, the company finds itself in serious financial difficulty, and many workers lose their jobs and insurance. The bottom has fallen out for them.

Many times there is no warning when the bottom falls out, no hint that the next day they will feel as though they have lost control of their lives and are falling into a bottomless black hole.

For people all across the country, the bottom fell out on September 11, 2001 in a way that no one could have imagined. It was a catastrophic tragedy of gigantic proportions, one that we have never before seen in our lifetime. It is so catastrophic that historians are saying now that the teenage generation will mark their era by it. It was the height of terrorism and the epitome of evil.

When people watched the events on television, it felt as though they were watching the latest Hollywood movie, it was so surreal. Buildings were shattered and came tumbling down. There was trouble everywhere. One young man yelled out, "I think this is Armageddon!" Thousands of innocent lives were lost. Within one hour, our country and the world had entered a new phase of its existence.

The Lord Is Our Strength

We are in the midst of a season of elevated chaos,

filled with confusion and great fear. We are now at war half way around the world. The 46th Psalm, however, reminds us that even in times of chaos, God remains our refuge: *"Therefore we will not fear, though the earth be removed, and though the mountains be carried into the midst of the sea."*

The Lord is the strength of our lives. Whom shall we fear? Of whom shall we be afraid? The Lord is our shield, our buckler, and our *strong* tower, unlike those which can be shattered. The Lord is our rock and our fortress! The Lord is our bridge over troubled waters! He is our shelter in the time of storm! The Lord is the strength of our lives!

Because of His power in us, we can take a stand together, overcome the spirit of fear, and declare that we shall not be afraid! We can find great assurance in the following familiar passages of scripture learned at our mother's knee...

The LORD is my shepherd; I shall not want. He maketh me to lie down in green pastures: he leadeth me beside the still waters. He restoreth my soul: he leadeth me in the paths of righteousness for his name's sake. Yea, though I walk through the valley of the shadow of death, I will fear no evil: for thou art with me; thy rod and thy staff they comfort me (Ps. 23:1-4).

God is our refuge and strength, a very present help in trouble. Therefore will not we fear, though the earth be removed, and though the mountains be carried into the midst of the sea; Though the waters thereof roar and be troubled, though the mountains shake with the swelling thereof. Selah. There is a river, the streams whereof shall make glad the city of God, the holy place of the tabernacles of the most High. God is in the midst of her; she shall not be moved: God shall help her, and that right early. The heathen raged, the kingdoms were moved: he uttered his voice, the earth melted. The LORD of hosts is with us; the God of Jacob is our refuge (Ps. 46:1-7).

Preparing for Trouble

It is unfortunate that we seem to only turn to Psalm 23 and others like it when we are in trouble. There are so many psalms that show us God's perspective about trouble, and we really need to read them *before* trouble comes. We need to have them chronicled in our mind so that we have a reserve of scriptures that speak to us about life-suffering seasons, seasons of persecution, and seasons of pain and grief.

Seasons will occur in our lives that will not make any sense to us. We are blessed to know, however, that God is working everything out for our good. There are some things that we may never understand, and yet, they will be made clear to us when we see God face to face.

We are pilgrims here on earth. All of our luxury cars, custom-made shoes, fancy houses and wonderful stock portfolios that we may have, will prove meaningless when we see the Lord face to face. They will hold no significance at all.

This kind of cataclysmic trouble has caused most of us to rethink our priorities and look at life differently. It helps us to put things in a better perspective. We understand that all of our running after money and what the world calls "success" is not really success at all in the eyes of God. Trouble helps us to put things in perspective and makes us realize the importance of things like love, family, friends, safety, and security.

Regardless of the troubles that we face in life, or the blessings God bestows upon us, He still remains our refuge and strength—not our money, stocks and bonds, or savings. God is always a present help in personal trouble. The same God, who is our refuge and our strength in times of personal trauma, is our refuge and our strength in times of national trauma. We are now in a season of national trauma, and people are pressing their way to the house of God.

Is There a Word From the Lord?

After September 11, people began pressing their way into churches across the country as never before. They were asking, "Is there a word from the Lord in these times?" Husbands, pregnant wives, children, mothers, fathers, brothers and sisters, thousands of them are dead. Even in the midst of all of this, even in the lessons that need to be learned, God is still God. He remains constant, caring, and concerned. His Word provides for the comfort we so desperately need these days and times. Horrific situations like this challenge us to look within the very core of our being and examine our faith and focus on life's eternal issues. The word from the Lord helps us find hope when we are hurting and provides us with courage to go on in spite of everything that has happened.

Fear is one of the most crippling afflictions of our day. We must not allow ourselves to become wrapped up in fear. These days it is a fight to keep fear from entering into our minds. Once fear is allowed to enter, however, it takes a firm grip on our minds, and without a doubt, we can become paralyzed by it. As God's people, we cannot allow such a thing to happen because we are His army for such a time as this.

The bottom line is that we do not have to walk in any kind of fear because God ultimately has the final say. Yes, in the end, right wins...light wins...love wins...God wins! In the meantime, however, we are all called to live our lives in a state of readiness and faith. *"So teach us to number our days, so that we may apply our hearts unto wisdom"* (Ps. 90:12).

Take some time to talk with God...
God hears!
Take some time to hear from God...
God speaks!

The Lord is my light and my salvation; whom shall I fear? The Lord is the strength of my life; of whom shall I be afraid?
Psalm 27:1

Chapter Two

How Does Tragedy Happen?

The psalmist speaks of a security that knows no walls that can be torn down, a security that knows no brick or mortar that can withstand the heat of the fires. He speaks of a security that does not have an earthly foundation from which it can be torn.

Our security lies in a river, and God is in that river. He shall help steady us and remain our refuge. Let the record be clear that terrorism does not change the fact that God is still our refuge.

Goodness may seem to be overcome for a season, but ultimately, right will always win out over wrong. Light cannot be swallowed up by the darkness. God has the last word! This is the faith we believe. God is always in control!

In the midst of trouble, God is still our refuge. We need to wrap the arms of our mind around that truth and believe it even when things happen in life that we cannot fully comprehend. Sad, indeed, are those who have no solid anchor of faith, especially in troubled times. We need to get a firm handle on God while we can because we do not know what the future holds. On September 10, 2001, the people working in the World Trade Center had no idea what would happen the very next day. As Christians, we know that God holds our future. Therefore, we can be at peace, knowing that He will always be God. Nothing can come to us, except it first be processed through divine love.

Evil Is Real

God's sovereign existence, however, does not negate the fact that evil does exist. Evil is real! Sometimes it has a face, hands, and feet. This was a calculated evil! Evil had a plan! Evil had blueprints! Evil had an agenda! Evil had a dream and vision! In fact, evil was so encumbered with its purpose that it was willing to die for it.

Evil planned that at a certain time on the 11th of September, four planes would be hijacked and used as instruments of terror. Evil convinced the perpetrators that even though there would be many innocent lives lost, they would be granted an immediate place in paradise when they perished on this perverted mission. We, of course, know they were deceived.

I am ashamed that sometimes evil is willing to die for its cause, yet some Christians are ashamed to stand up and risk embarrassment for the cause of Christ who died to save us from the wages of sin and to deliver us from evil. I am ashamed at how evil speedily follows through with its agenda while we remain too often divided. Evil is set at conquering the lives of our children, taking control of our schools, and infiltrating our homes because it is willing to go to any lengths to fulfill its purpose.

What we saw on the 11th of September was consummate evil. It went beyond the demonic things that we talk about in the church. It was "high-powered evil," wickedness in high places. It was something more than our simplistic, animated images of the devil in a red suit, with a pitchfork and long, pointed tail. It was planned, calculated, and horrific evil. Every time they showed the towers falling, we wanted to shout, "How could anyone do this?"

This act was heightened, diabolical, demonic infiltration instigated by the devil. It was evil with a face and a strong determination. So many of us attempt something once, and if it does not immediately work out, we give up. Terrorism is not easily discouraged, however. Terrorism is calculated evil with a purpose in mind—success at any price!

Not God's Design

The question on many people's minds is, "Was this God's design?" No! God will allow some things to happen in our lives, but everything that happens to us is not by His design. Evil has done this! Only a demon could orchestrate in its mind evil of this kind of magnitude. Thousands of innocent people who routinely awakened and made their way to work or who boarded an airplane are now dead as a result.

It is good to know, however, that God brings something good out of even the most horrific circumstances. Many times we may not fully understand everything that has occurred, and yet, *"we know that all things work together for good to them that love God, to them who are the called according to his purpose"* (Ro. 8:28). Even in the midst of evil, we can be sure there will be a word from the Lord.

In Psalm 27, the psalmist boldly declares faith and a confidence in the midst of confusion. With an exuberant declaration of faith, he reminds us that the Lord is our light and salvation. The Lord is our direction, and He is our salvation. Therefore, whom shall we fear and under what circumstances shall we be afraid? We know, unequivocally, that He is always with us.

We need to walk in confidence so that, as we go forward, we will not do so in fear but rather in faith. The word from the Lord is that God is still a good God! God is still an awesome God! God is still the Alpha and the Omega! He is the great I AM! He is still the God who will make a way out of no way. He is Jehovah Jireh! Our God is yet alive! Therefore, whom shall we fear?

Remind yourself on a daily basis…

I WILL NOT FEAR!

One thing have I desired of the LORD, that
will I seek after; that I may dwell in the
house of the LORD all the days of my life,
to behold the beauty of the LORD, and to
enquire in his temple.
Psalm 27:4

Chapter Three

Why Does Tragedy Happen?

We saw a display of wickedness on September 11, 2001 unlike any that our nation has ever witnessed. To this day, many mourn and grieve the loss of thousands of lives. Although it may not have been widely expressed, many were angry. I found myself torn between anger and grief each time I saw the events replayed on the television. I thought about how many young widows and their children sat in the front rows of churches all across America. How many parents lost their children, some of whom may have just graduated from college and were ready to begin a new life?

I was angry because of the senseless loss of life. Life will never be the same again for any of us. My children will not grow up with the innocence of life with which I did. I was angry because every time I saw a plane flying over, I remembered what had happened. I was angry because of a sense of fear that I must deal with and now speak against on a daily basis. Concerned, angry, confused, disturbed, and grieved, but not overcome. No, we will not be overcome with fear! We don't always understand why tragedy happens. We must, however, place our trust in the God who is able to carry us through our pain and suffering to victory. Yes, so many people died. Did they deserve such a death? No! Was God, however, with them? Yes! In the midst of that destruction, God was there. Our comfort is that those who belong to God are now in His loving arms.

Sometimes God Uses Suffering As a Witness

Sometimes God uses our suffering and bloodshed as a testimony. Look at the great martyrs of the faith. Their greatest witness was the blood that they willingly shared for their faith. Look at the priest who died at the Trade Center. He died giving the last rites to a fireman. What a way to leave this world, praying for and ministering to someone else! This priest willingly gave his life while praying for his brother. *"Greater love hath no man than this, that a man lay down his life for his friends"* (Jn. 15:13).

Although God did not orchestrate this tragedy, He did allow it. It, then, becomes our purpose to understand His will in the midst of tragedies. We must ask ourselves, "What is God trying to say in this situation?"

Tragedy helps us put things in perspective. One of the things we see happening now in the aftermath of the tragedy is that people are coming together in unprecedented ways, regardless of their skin color or background. Cultures are coming together and working together side-by-side. The blood that was shed, whether at the World Trade Center Towers, the Pentagon, or in Pennsylvania, was red. One of the lessons that we need to learn from this tragedy is that we need to adjust our priorities. Prior to this tragedy, many of us failed to spend quality time with loved ones on a regular basis. Afterwards, however, we saw a boost in sales for family board games and family structured activities. We learned from this tragedy that family matters!

Turn to God for Peace

For a period of time after the tragedy, we were packed in churches like sardines. Many people, who had previously never thought about God, all of a sudden found themselves—every race, nationality, and ethnicity—bowing down to Him. Why did they come? They came in search of peace.

Many of us are angry because we know that the terrorists' attack was not right or justifiable. The greatest tragedy is that everyone that perished that morning did nothing more than get up and go to work to take care of their families or to board an airplane. The policemen and firefighters did nothing wrong. They went into the burning buildings to help other people and ultimately lost their lives in the process. The priest who was giving the last rites to a fireman lost his life. Innocent people died that day. Senseless bloodshed took place on that September morning, a morning none of us will every forget.

The Bible declares that in the last days there will be all kinds of strange, catastrophic things happening. There will be wars and rumors of wars. Following this tragedy, we need to turn to God in order to deal with it and with what lies ahead for us. Who knows what tomorrow will bring? And yet, we know who holds our future.

One of our church members had several friends that worked on the top floor and was concerned that they had all perished. A couple of our members had relatives there. Another member's husband was there at a breakfast meeting. All of these people needed peace, but how could they find it? In situations like this, we need supernatural intervention. It takes more than Valium, a shot of gin or whiskey, or marijuana to help us get through times like these. Many people have found solace in alcohol or drugs, but they were only temporary fixes. We need a supernatural impartation of the Holy Ghost to breathe on us to speak a word into our spirits in times like these.

The scripture says in 2 Chronicles 7:14,

> *If my people, which are called by my name, shall humble themselves, and pray, and seek my face, and turn from their wicked ways; then will I hear from heaven, and will forgive their sin, and will heal their land.*

This means we must call on God and take Him seriously. Empty promises that we will straighten out our lives if He will help us in a crisis are, indeed, meaningless. I have often told my congregation that it is better to "have Christ and not need Him than to need Him and not have Him." We should know the Lord in times of peace before a crisis enters our lives.

I am sure that there were very few people cursing God on that Tuesday morning. Many were running for their lives, calling on the name of Jesus for help. God wants us to confess our faults and bring our needs to Him. Furthermore, He requires that His Spirit penetrates our hearts so that our ethics, habits, politics, and justice line up with His will. Then we shall find true peace in God.

Tragedies will happen, but God is always there to catch us when the bottom falls out!

Have you made peace with God?
Once you do, you can overcome your fear
of death...you are truly free.

---

*For in the time of trouble He shall hide me
in His pavilion: in the secret of His
tabernacle shall He hide me; He shall set
me up upon a rock.*
Psalm 27:5

Chapter Four

Why?

One question that has come up repeatedly since the September 11 tragedy concerns biblical prophecy. Was this a foretaste of Armageddon? People have also asked questions such as, "If it is true that God has plans for us that are good and not for evil, how could people of purpose die in this disaster?" "Why did God let me live when other co-workers died?" "How does this event relate to purpose and how does it relate to destiny?"

Great care must be taken in answering such weighty questions. There are no quick or easy answers to them. One also must guard against exploiting tragedy to push a certain agenda. Far too many Christian leaders were offering responses to this tragedy that were insensitive and incorrect.

Many people may not have an understanding of "Armageddon." In a nutshell, Armageddon is the final war between good and evil described in the book of Revelation. In that book, God not only gives us a wonderful picture of what heaven will look like, but also a foretaste of the last battle and the sign of the times in which it will occur.

Now I believe that Scripture says that the church will be "caught up" in the Rapture before the War of Armageddon occurs. However, I also believe that the Trade Center crashes and the highjackings all line up with the calamity, chaos, and the stage that is being set for the coming of the Lord. Now the comfort that we have is that whether or not we are snatched out of the earth with the coming of the Lord before Armageddon, the final war, or the great tribulation, we are with God. The Scriptures tell us that whether we live or whether we die, we will be with the Lord. In the same vein, whether we go through the end war, or whether we are snatched away, we belong to the Lord. He will come *with* us, or He will come *for* us. When He comes to set up His kingdom, we will be with Him. Whether we are there before or after, God is still our refuge. He shall *always* be our refuge.

The Restraint of the Holy Spirit

We need to be comforted with the fact that as long as there are saints in the earth, there is the restraining power of the Holy Spirit. Some Bible scholars suggest that during the time of tribulation, complete lawlessness and chaos will be prevalent because the power and the presence of the Holy Spirit will have been taken out of the earth. Because the Holy Spirit resides in the saints of God, when the saints are snatched away, the earth will be void of the Holy Spirit and there will be an unleashing of evil.

The events of September 11 are only a foretaste of the unleashing of evil that is to come. This means that we should not take for granted the hope of glory within us. The Scriptures teach us that we are temples of the Holy Spirit. The question could be asked, "If this is so, then what happened to those who had the Holy Spirit and died in the towers?" When we are snatched out of the earth, so also will be the power and presence of the Holy Spirit, who is the restrainer of evil. We do not teach much about Him being the restrainer. We teach that He is the comforter, enabler, baptizer, and convicter of sin, but the Holy Spirit is also a restrainer of evil. The power that lies within you is both a blessing and a hope for you when you are in your neighborhood, on the street, or on your job. Evil can only go but so far. Do not take for granted the anointing, glory, and hope that lies within you.

There Is Comfort

Even in the midst of chaos, the saints of God can be comforted in the knowledge that He is coming for His own. Matthew 24 talks about the fact that near the end times there will be wars and rumors of wars. So, we see that the stage is being set today. It is not the time for

Armageddon yet, but the stage is being set for the consummation of all things. Should we be afraid? No, but we are to keep our lamps trimmed and burning. Every one of us should live our lives in readiness until He comes. Our Lord teaches in Matthew 25:13, *"Watch therefore, for ye know neither the day nor the hour wherein the Son of man cometh."* We are also called to be salt and light to the world.

> *You are the salt of the earth. But if the salt loses its saltiness, how can it be made salty again? It is no longer good for anything, except to be thrown out and trampled by men. You are the light of the world. A city on a hill cannot be hidden. Neither do people light a lamp and put it under a bowl. Instead they put it on its stand, and it gives light to everyone in the house. In the same way, let your light shine before men, that they may see your good deeds and praise your Father in heaven* (Matt. 5:13-16).

We are called to help light the way for others through how we live our lives. If people around us are stumbling in the darkness, they will respond to our light and want to find its source.

There are some things for which there will be no justifiable explanation in this life. As I mentioned before, when we get to heaven there will be a vast multitude of people with their hands raised, wanting to have answers for some questions that were never appropriately answered in this life. When the Bible states that the just should live by faith, we always thought that it meant faith for healing or faith to have money or success or prosperity. What it means, however, is that the just shall live "in faith" even when everything around us is crumbling. The faithful always find a place of solace and strength even in the midst of calamity. Our faith, assurance, and commitment to the God who remains our rock and our help will remain strong. This is our true strength. Even when everything around us is in chaos, we will not fall when we live by faith.

Constant Readiness

In Matthew 25:1-13, we read,

Then the kingdom of heaven shall be likened to the ten virgins who took their lamps and went out to meet the bridegroom. Now five were foolish and five were wise and those who were foolish took their lamps and took no oil with them. But the wise took their oil and their vessels with their lamps. But while the bridegroom was delayed, they all slumbered and slept.

I believe that many people were sleeping on September 11, 2001, even those who are true believers in God. The scripture continues,

And at midnight a cry went out "Behold the bridegroom cometh, come and meet him." And all the virgins arose and trimmed their lamps

*and the foolish said to the wise, give us some of
your oil, for our lamps are going out.*

In the midst of tragedy, people say, "Let us have
some of your anointing, some of your prayer life, some
of your consecration, and some of your fire." They were
pleading, "Let us sing some of your songs and let us have
some of your peace."

While some were sitting, feasting at His table and understanding how to deepen their relationship with Him,
others were foolish because they thought they had more
time. None of us knows how much time we have.
Therefore, we must live each day to the fullest with our
eyes focused on our divine purpose.

Is your lamp burning out? Maybe you are singing in
the choir every Sunday, yet your lamp is burning out.
Maybe you hold an ordained position as a leader, and
yet, the flame in your lamp is burning low. Jesus wants
to know if your lamp is "trimmed and burning" or is it
just plain *burning out*?

When the five foolish virgins went to get more oil for
their lamps,

*And while they went to buy, the bridegroom
came; and they that were ready went in with
him to the marriage: and the door was shut.
Afterward came also the other virgins, saying,
Lord, Lord, open to us. But he answered and
said, Verily I say unto you, I know you not.
Watch therefore, for ye know neither the day nor
the hour wherein the Son of man cometh* (Matt.
24:10-13).

We are to live our lives in complete obedience to God and not be intimidated by evil. We are to live our lives with an attitude of repentance and holy reverence for God. We are to walk in peace with our neighbor and treat others as we want to be treated. We are to live our lives as if tomorrow may be our last because it just might be. However, we are not to be afraid of the future but live in spiritual readiness and enjoy our lives in Him.

All that we do must encompass Him. We are to live our lives in readiness, and be prepared to be the salt of the earth and the light of the world.

The question becomes, "Will we be ready when Jesus comes?" When Armageddon occurs, there will be great chaos...screams and blood, torment and pain, scars and earthquakes, mourning, and sorrows upon sorrows. What we witnessed on September 11 was only a foretaste of that great and terrible day, which will mark the final war between good and evil.

Before that day, there will be other challenges—both small and great—in our lives. Who knows if and when the terrorists will attack again? While we try to prepare for the possibility, if the unthinkable happens again, where will our comfort lie? The only firm foundation we can build our lives upon is our relationship to Almighty God. The book of Revelation speaks of the victory that we shall have in Him and how good ultimately triumphs over evil. We shall experience the final victory!

Are you prepared in the event of future calamity? Physical preparedness will not take the place of spiritual readiness.

God is our refuge and strength, a very present help in trouble. Therefore will not we fear, though the earth be removed, and though the mountains be carried into the midst of the sea; Though the waters thereof roar and be troubled, though the mountains shake with the swelling thereof.
Psalm 46:1-3

Chapter Five

What Is God Saying to Us Now?

We know that God is our refuge, strength, and hope. In these days, we are especially hopeful for an end to terrorism and that God will heal our land so we will all walk together in peace. How will this happen? It cannot happen without God's wisdom and direction.

Indeed, we need direction today and in the days ahead. Our president and legislature need direction. The police and fire departments need direction. Preachers and prophets need direction. Priests and rabbis need direction. We are all in need of the Lord's wisdom, guidance, and directive hand.

What is the Lord saying to the nation and to us individually? Other nations have experienced far worse over the centuries. Just think about the devastation in Europe during the World Wars. America has been so blessed throughout its short history. We tend to take this for granted. Not anymore! Our national safety is no longer guaranteed.

Many Americans still ask the question, "How could this happen to us? Why does God let bad things happen to good people?" Of course, there is no easy answer that we can give. The psalmist sought the same answer centuries ago in Psalm 73:17.

When I thought to know this, it was too painful for me; Until I went into the sanctuary of God; then understood I their end.

In this passage, David was expressing his frustration at seeing the wicked prosper and go unpunished. It was only when he went into the sanctuary and focused on God that he was able to understand that ultimately, we will reap what we sow. Right will always triumph over evil in the end!

Paul contends that there is a comfort that can only come from God. "Blessed be the God, even the Father of our Lord Jesus Christ, the Father of mercies, and the God of all comfort" (2 Co. 1:3). He is our comfort. Many of us have pressed our way into the presence of God these days because we need to be calmed by the comfort that only the Holy Spirit can give us. As David did, we need a word of comfort in the midst of our confusion over the iniquity and consummate evil manifested through terrorism.

God Is Trying To Tell Us Something

Several movies scheduled to be released around September 11 were postponed. Indeed, they were deemed to contain too much violence or were too closely related to the tragedy. Perhaps God is trying to tell us, "Wake up! If it was too violent then, it is too violent to watch now." It is quite possible that we have become too comfortable with violence. Even children's cartoons and video games have become so violent that we must take steps to oversee them. Many schools have almost come to the point of needing metal detectors at their doors to prevent furthers tragedies such as the Columbine murders.

While in the case of tragedies such as these, God does not send evil upon us but rather allows even our calamities to work together for our good. While He neither caused the 9-11 nor the Columbine tragedies, He does have an ultimate purpose that He is working out through them.

God is concerned with how we live and how we are raising our children. He desires to speak to the nation. Some things we may never fully understand, but we do know that He is sovereign and is ultimately in control even when everything may suggest that He is not.

"Speak to my heart," is what I ask of the Lord. "Help me do what I am supposed to do, when I am supposed to do it. Help me not to harbor malice in my heart."

Of course, God's concern reaches beyond this nation. God's sovereignty spans the Soviet Union, Angola,

Japan, Jerusalem as well as Harlem. He is God in Los Angeles, and at the same time, He is God in Anchorage, Alaska, and in San Antonio, Texas. He speaks to all of us, and we must learn to listen to what He has to say.

We serve a great, sovereign God. Even in the midst of tragedy, we can proclaim that He is an awesome God who reigns, rules, and lives. I, for one, am so glad that I know Him.

God uses various things to bring us to Himself and to humble us before Him. He uses broken marriages, messed up love affairs, broken hearts, lost jobs, and even loneliness. We may not even remember what it was, but God used something to draw every one of us to Himself. Why then cannot God use what happened on that fateful Tuesday morning to draw us back to the altar and our nation back to Him?

Time to Seek His Face

It is time to pray and to open the Word to see what God has to reveal about Himself, His universe, and our future.

If my people, which are called by my name, shall humble themselves, and pray, and seek my face, and turn from their wicked ways; then will I hear from heaven, and will forgive their sin, and will heal their land.(2 Ch. 7:14).

We need to seek His revelation, His will, His peace, His comfort, His strength, His joy, and above all, His face. "Lord, help us to understand Your will for our lives. Help us not to forget that You placed us here at this season for a purpose. Help us to seek Your face daily as You order the steps in our lives."

In fact, in the grand scheme of things, it is not asking too much that I attend church, worship God, obey Him, and thank Him for my life. Giving thanks to God is a good place to begin as we seek to humble ourselves and understand what He is saying to us.

Right now is a good time to thank God that you are alive. Pray over your children... thank God for them...give His name praise.

Though the waters thereof roar and be troubled, though the mountains shake with the swelling thereof. Selah. There is a river, the streams whereof shall make glad the city of God, the holy place of the tabernacles of the most High.
Psalm 46:3-4

Chapter Six

What Can We Learn From Tragedy?

Divine love calls us to identify with other people's pain. Tragedy leaves people broken, hurting, and in need of comfort. Romans 12:15 exhorts us to "Rejoice with them that do rejoice, and weep with them that weep."

I will never forget the day when I was young in the Lord, and attended the funeral of a woman's son. The choir and praise team sang during the service. The praise team sang, "Look and See What God Has Done." This hymn offered absolutely no comfort during such a time. More appropriate would have been a song with comforting words such as, "Precious Lord, take my hand, lead me on, let me stand. I am tired, I am weak, I am worn. Through the storm, through the night, lead me on, to the light. Savior, take my hand, precious Lord, lead me on."

Great sensitivity is needed during seasons of grief. As Christians, we must have compassion on others. When in doubt about what to say, it is always better to say nothing and offer our support to the grieving person. Your presence alone is all some people may need.

Death Is Not the End

After the attacks on the World Trade Center, we saw a myriad of names of those who perished in the tragedy. One couple, killed in the Pennsylvania plane crash, were leaders of a Bible study group in South Jersey. These Christian soldiers died in faith. Like most of us, I claim long life for my family members and those with whom I remain close. However, many of us need a more proper understanding of death.

As Christians, we know that death is not the end and that we need to share that message with others. The bodies of those who knew Him may have been lost on that day, but right now, their souls are in the presence of God. They are whole and at peace.

Although it may not seem logical to some, heaven is still our home, and death is not the end! This life is not all there is. There is a place that the saints call home. Job declared that in that place, "the wicked will cease from troubling us and the weary soul will be at rest." As Christians, we need to think more about heaven, not in morbid terms, but rather as a wonderful continuation of life.

In my African-American tradition, the preachers years ago talked about heaven in most of their sermons. They would end with, "One of these old days, it will not be long; you are going to look for me and I will be gone. Going up to heaven to sing and shout; there will be nobody there that can put me out." In some cases, there was too much focus on life after death, and too little focus on the abundant life on earth. I feel that the opposite is the case now. Our focus tends to be on education, job status, physical fitness, and our appearance. We need, however, a healthy balance of the good life here and now as well as our eternal home in heaven.

Turn Toward God

What can we learn from tragedy in this life? Sometimes, God uses tragedy to get our attention so that we can make a deliberate decision to turn toward Him. In some cases, we turn toward Him only after we have exhausted every other alternative.

After this tragedy, many of us saw a great need for another place of rest, another word of revelation because our old ones were not good enough anymore. Some who used to find rest in the tavern cannot find peace there any more. Others, who used to find rest in their stock portfolios cannot find it by looking over them anymore. Still others cannot find rest in shining their cars or being on the golf course on Sunday. Those things seem empty in light of the death and devastation of the terrorists' attacks on us. We are all reexamining our priorities.

In difficult times, we need to have a solid anchor and to be rooted in the Word of God. Because life is short, we need a clearer focus on what is really important in life.

Adjust Our Priorities

As a nation, we need to adjust our priorities. We have become greedy, materialistic, and desensitized to violence. I mentioned before about the many movies and programs that could not air immediately after this tragedy because of their violent content. If it was too violent to air *after* the tragedy, it should have been too violent to air *before* the tragedy. Maybe God is trying to address how comfortable we have become with violence in this country. While the attacks on the World Trade Center were the results of international terrorism, there is local and neighborhood terrorism happening in the streets of our cities, suburbs, and towns. God is speaking a word to the nation in these times: "America, adjust your priorities, stop the glorification of violence, and remember to put God first!"

Addressing Our Arrogance

Next, I believe that we need to address our own *arrogance* as a nation. The Lord is in control of this nation. It is He who holds it together, not military might, as some may suspect. Yes, we are a proud people, and thank God we are a free people. We can choose our own praying ground, we have the right to vote, and we can be educated. Sadly, however, we have become gods unto ourselves and have forgotten our God who is the "Rock of Ages." Isaac Watts' hymn, "O God Our Help in Ages Past," is a paraphrase of Psalm 90.

O GOD, OUR HELP IN AGES PAST

O God, our help in ages past,
Our hope for years to come,
Our shelter from the stormy blast,
And our eternal home

Under the shadow of Thy throne
Still may we dwell secure;
Sufficient is Thine arm alone,
And our defense is sure.

We also must address our own individual arrogance. Too often, we think of ourselves as better than others. We look down on those who are on welfare, the home- less, and unwed mothers. We must learn to walk with humility.

In Psalm 51, David says, as a result of his sin, "Against thee, oh God, only have I sinned." David was saying, in essence, "Lord, help me deal with my own heart before I start pointing a finger at other people. Help me deal with the areas that I need to have ad- dressed in my own life." In a nutshell, we need to "Do unto others as we would have others to do unto us."

Our Distance From God

I observed with great interest how our nation wor- shiped God, bowed down in prayer, and wiped their eyes in sorrow. I listened as Billy Graham at the National Cathedral in Washington D.C., unashamedly called us back to God. Tragic circumstances forced us to our knees before an all-caring, all-wise God.

We must confess our sins and realize how far we have moved away from God. Elisha Hoffman, in the fourth verse of his classic hymn, "I Must Tell Jesus," says it best...

I MUST TELL JESUS
O how the world to evil allures me!
O how my heart is tempted to sin!
I must tell Jesus, and He will help me
Over the world the vict'ry to win.

There are so many distractions that move us away from God. We choose positions, power, and prestige, only to find out that they do not bring long-term satisfaction. Money can make life more comfortable, however, it may not necessarily make it more gratifying. True satisfaction comes from within. Once we reconnect with and relate to our Creator, we will grow in peace. Contentment is a result of a soul at peace with God and within itself. Such deep and abiding satisfaction simply cannot be found in circumstances or material things, all of which can change at a moment's notice. Peace can come from Him and Him alone!

Now is the time to reevaluate and ask ourselves, "Am I anchored in God? Do I have an eternal home in the heavens not made by hands?" We need the full assurance that causes us to remain resilient in the time of a crisis. If we lose our jobs, He's God anyhow. In the midst of your personal crisis, He is God. In personal bankruptcy, He is God. In the midst of chemotherapy, He is God. In the midst of going to the courtroom, He is God. He is God in the jailhouse and in the intensive care unit. If Wall Street were to crash tomorrow, He would still be God!

I have found fresh comfort in that familiar passage found in Romans 8:35-39:

Who shall separate us from the love of Christ? shall tribulation, or distress, or persecution, or famine, or nakedness, or peril, or sword? As it is written, For thy sake we are killed all the day long; we are accounted as sheep for the slaughter. Nay, in all these things we are more than conquerors through him that loved us. For I am persuaded, that neither death, nor life, nor angels, nor principalities, nor powers, nor things present, nor things to come, Nor height, nor depth, nor any other creature, shall be able to separate us from the love of God, which is in Christ Jesus our Lord.

Can Heaven Wait?

There is a great deal of "heaven talk" these days. Not long ago, baby boomers and the X-generation did not care to discuss heaven. After all, we do all we can to live well here. Sadly, however, the majority of those who perished on September 11, 2001 were 25–45 years old.

They were gone overnight, leaving everything behind. Some even had pregnant wives at home.

What are some of the lessons we can learn during these times? We are called to...

Adjust our priorities...

Admit our sins...

Arise in faith and...

Accept His divine love.

Matthew 11:28 says, "Come unto me, all ye that labour and are heavy laden, and I will give you rest." I have a residence waiting for me in heaven. The old folks from down south used to say, "I've got my ticket in my hand. I'm on my way. I'm going to see Jesus." We need to remember there is a new heaven and a new earth coming.

> What lessons have you learned through tragedies in your life?

Therefore if any man be in Christ, he is a new creature: old things are passed away; behold, all things are become new.
2 Corinthians 5:17

Chapter Seven

How Then Shall We Live?

After any major tragedy, we must somehow find the strength to carry on with our everyday lives and fulfill our responsibilities. No matter how broken and torn apart we may feel, we still must do it. Isaiah 40 and 60 speak to us about a broken people, the Israelites, who were in exile. They were in mourning, raw with grief, and overcome by loss. In chapter 40, Isaiah brought a clear message of hope to them when he said...

Comfort ye, comfort ye my people, saith your God. Speak ye comfortably to Jerusalem, and cry unto her, that her warfare is accomplished, that her iniquity is pardoned: for she hath received of the LORD'S hand double for all her sins. The voice of him that crieth in the wilderness, Prepare ye the way of the LORD, make straight in the desert a highway for our God. Every valley shall be exalted, and every mountain and hill shall be made low: and the crooked shall be made straight, and the rough places plain: that an hour was coming where every valley would be exalted and every crooked place made straight (Is. 40:1-4).

Isaiah wanted to refocus Israel's attention on the mercy of God and help them see beyond their present grief. When the Messiah comes, we will see that God has been sovereign all along. In the midst of a storm, we sometimes ask God, "Why would you allow us to suffer? What is the meaning of so much pain?"

Isaiah spoke to people who were exhausted with grief, suffering, and pain. Suffering for a long time can make you weary and anxious. Intense suffering wears on one's senses and makes ordinary tasks appear monumental.

Isaiah instructed them that there was more to life than their present circumstances. Today we need to know there is something else beyond our present pain and loss; there is life beyond our present suffering.

Many of us have tried to manufacture excitement, family love, good feelings, and happiness The end result, however, is more debt as a result of trying to dig our way out of what we attempted to manufacture. Many times, this is the direct result of not being able to squarely confront our losses.

What Isaiah is trying to say in Chapter 40 is that we have to learn how to come to God and call on Him who is able to keep us from falling. We must give Him the opportunity to change our focus. He will not force His will on anyone. We have to want His will for our lives and ask Him to open our eyes that we may see beyond our circumstances. That is the challenge.

Many of us are consumed with pain and have not learned how to manage it. There may be things that we will never fully understand, but they should not continue to plague us in the same way they did years before. As we grow in Christ, our ability to handle the crises in our lives should grow as well.

We need to say, "God, help us close the door on this pain. We need to know that You are concerned about our pain and want to help us resolve it. We trust You completely to straighten out the crooked places in our lives."

A Word of Comfort

Isaiah promises us that God will, indeed, comfort us. The first two verses of Chapter 40 encourage us, *"Comfort, comfort my people, says your God. Speak tenderly to Jerusalem."* In the same way that Isaiah spoke comfort to Israel, we need to speak comfort to others, especially in the midnight hours of a tragedy. All over the nation, people are trying to grab hold of something tangible to get them through this crisis. People everywhere are attempting to find threads of peace to comfort them.

We must believe Isaiah 60:1, *"Arise, shine; for thy*

light is come, and the glory of the LORD is risen upon thee." Isaiah is prophesying about a light that is to come, and speaking things that were not yet as though they already were. In other words, we can rejoice and be glad because the Light, our Savior, has already come. The Light of Christ, born more than 2,000 years ago, is still being revealed today. His light is still shining and will never be overcome by the darkness. God wants His people to be comforted with the knowledge that He still lives and reigns and is concerned about the dark places in our lives. Even though the bottom appears to have fallen out, God remains the same. He is always there for us.

God's Salvation Has Come

God's salvation has already come. The Messiah has come. This is our faith, and this is what we believe. Jesus is God Almighty! He was born of a virgin, wrapped in swaddling clothes, laid in a manger, suffered, bled, and died for our sins, was buried and rose again on the third day with all power in His hand. Our challenge, then, is to lift our sights above what we see in the natural and trust God's divine plan for our lives.

It costs us something to confront our losses. For many of us, this has been a season of loss in our lives. Some may have lost jobs, our standard of living, and money in the stock market. Others have lost loved ones, family, friends, or acquaintances.

Have you confronted those areas of loss in your life for which you mourn? As Isaiah says in the 60th chapter, we must arise because we are summoned by God to do so. Know that God has already provided the comfort we need to do so. When we receive it, we can then move forward.

What has God summoned you to do?
Take some time and think about areas of
your life that may appear dark to you right
now. Take those things and lay them at the
altar of God and know that
He will comfort and enlighten you.

Arise, shine; for thy light is come, and the glory of the LORD is risen upon thee. For, behold, the darkness shall cover the earth, and gross darkness the people: but the LORD shall arise upon thee, and his glory shall be seen upon thee. And the Gentiles shall come to thy light, and kings to the brightness of thy rising.
Psalm 60:1-3

Chapter Eight

Be Grateful!

After the attacks on the World Trade Center, I read a comment in the newspaper by a woman who said that she did not know how to face Thanksgiving, having lost her husband in the attack. She cried, "I do not have anything for which to give God thanks!" The next issue, however, gave the testimony of another woman who replied, "I, too, lost my husband in the attacks and for that I am sorry, but I want to thank and praise God that my husband left me with five beautiful children. I am also pregnant right now. I have everything to be thankful for. I may not have my husband, but I have my children. I have to give God thanks for what I have left."

Even after suffering a great loss, we still must thank Him for what we have left. God can take what we have and multiply it. That is why it is so important for us to stay connected to God and His power.

Although we mourned together as a nation, in the midst of it all, we must pause and give God thanks. "Thank You for making a way out of no way. Thank You for being God! Thank You for keeping our heads above the water. Thank You for not allowing us to be consumed by our circumstances." Thank God for what you have left. Job declared that he would give the Lord thanks in all things. We should feel that way as well.

The Lord gave, and the Lord hath taken away;
blessed be the name of the Lord (Job 1:21).

The Power of Gratitude

There are all kinds of people in the world, but in this section, I want to focus primarily on two groups—those who are thankful and those who are not. Some people take notice of the small things in life. No matter what you do for them, regardless of how insignificant, they are grateful. Then there are those for whom you can never do enough. No matter how much you sacrifice, it is never enough. This kind of person never takes the time to acknowledge anything that is done for them. "Thank you" never crosses their lips.

All of us need to be thankful. There is real power resident in such an attitude. An old woman told me years ago, "Honey, good manners will take you where money cannot." We need to stop long enough to acknowledge

God and say, "Lord, I want to thank You for the things that I so often take for granted—my life, health, and strength."

Years ago, our elders would rise during testimony services on Wednesday nights and testify of the goodness of the Lord. "I want to thank and praise God for the clothes on my back and a roof over my head." Why is it then that we do not take the time to thank Him in the same way now? We do not pause long enough to thank God for anything even though we own far more than our elders did at that time. Have you ever stopped to think about how many people go to bed hungry and cold? We take too much for granted in our society today.

We are challenged by the 92nd Psalm to give God praise for His love and faithfulness. This is considered a psalm of thanksgiving and often shared by the people of God during worship services. As they came to worship, one of the leaders would read, "It is a good thing to give thanks unto the Lord...to give Him praise, to give Him glory and to sing praises unto His name, oh, Most High."

The Scriptures teach us that God wants His people to be appreciative, gracious, and above all, thankful. We are to be thankful more than just one day out of the year on Thanksgiving. We are to live our daily lives with an attitude of gratitude. Even during those seasons when we are experiencing great pain, God is still loving us. We must continue to thank Him in spite of our pain.

In November 2001, as I sat down at the table on Thanksgiving Day, my mind went to a text that I had been meditating on all week. Deuteronomy 8:15-18 says it was God...

Who led thee through that great and terrible wilderness, wherein were fiery serpents, and scorpions, and drought, where there was no water; who brought thee forth water out of the rock of flint; Who fed thee in the wilderness with manna, which thy fathers knew not, that he might humble thee, and that he might prove thee, to do thee good at thy latter end; And thou say in thine heart, My power and the might of mine hand hath gotten me this wealth. But thou shalt remember the LORD thy God: for it is he that giveth thee power to get wealth, that he may establish his covenant which he sware unto thy fathers, as it is this day.

I wanted to take the time to reflect on my own life about all of the things for which I was grateful. In Psalm 137, verse 6 reads, "If I do not remember thee, let my tongue cleave to the roof of my mouth." I do not want to fail to pause and say, "Thank you, Lord," or be like one of the ungrateful nine lepers that Jesus healed. Only one leper returned to say, "I want to give you thanks and praise because I was bound by leprosy. You laid your hand on me and I was healed."

Paul exhorts the Thessalonians, "In everything give thanks" (I Thess. 5:18). Notice that it does not say "for everything," but rather, "in everything." We do not thank God for evil, but we thank God that even in the midst of evil and terrorism, He is still in control! So we do not thank God *for* everything, but *in* everything we give thanks.

For Favor...

Therefore, on that Thanksgiving Day, I looked around the table, and I thanked God *for favor*. I thanked God that I had a roof over my head and food on the table. I thanked God that I had a table on which to put the food and a floor on which to put the table. I thanked Him that I was able to sit down on my own and even for the chair on which I sat. There are so many people that have no place to live, let alone sit on Thanksgiving Day.

Not long ago, I saw a young man with whom I went to high school. He was living on the street in the train station. He and I had attended school together, and yet, there he was: toothless, emaciated, and in a food line. Why the difference between us? It was certainly not because of my own goodness. It was the favor of God on my life. I have learned that one of the secrets of walking with God's favor is to walk in gratitude. To be thankful and to remember not to take little things for granted is critical. I thank God for favor.

For Food...

Next, I thanked God *for food*. I thanked Him for food because there were many people on that day who did not have any food. There were many people who were eating their Thanksgiving dinner on the streets and finding their food in a garbage can. So many of us throw away more food in one day than some people may eat in a week. It is a good thing to give thanks unto the Lord for food.

For Family...

I thanked God *for family*. I thanked Him especially for family after memorializing two of my own church members after the World Trade Center attacks. I took the time to remember their families on that day. I thanked God that I, myself, did not die. I thanked God that He chose to spare my life and the lives of those I love. I could have been in the World Trade Center on that day. In fact, I was there just a couple of months before giving a speech. I could have been there at that exact time, but through God's mercy I was not. I am more grateful than ever for my family.

I thanked Him for a good wife and three healthy children, a mother, sister, niece, two nephews, and a mother-in-law who all sat around the table that day. As I paused to give God thanks, we took hands and prayed. I was emotionally overwhelmed to the point that I went into another room, bowed down over the sink, and wept, not tears of sorrow, but tears of thanksgiving. I wept and prayed, "Thank You for my wife, children, family, and home." Indeed, the psalmist says it is a good thing for us to give thanks unto God. Psalm 103 exhorts us to bless the Lord and remember the God who "heals all of our diseases and who satisfies our thirsty souls."

For Friends...

I thanked God *for friends*...special friends from all across the country who support me throughout the year. Several of the pastors, to whom I serve as their bishop, called to wish me "Happy Thanksgiving." Proverbs 17:17

states, "A friend loveth at all times." A true friend is genuinely excited about your successes in life. A true friend can genuinely rejoice when you are blessed. A true friend is concerned when you are sick or in trouble. Therefore, on this day, I thanked God for friends.

For a Right Frame of Mind...

I thanked God for a right *frame of mind*. I thanked Him that I had the mind to appreciate who and where I was. There are many people who no longer have the capability of knowing who they are. Pressures and troubles in life can cause even a stable mind to falter. Yes, I, like many, do not always "feel sane," but I am most grateful that I am, indeed, "clothed in my right mind."

For Faith...

I thanked God *for faith*. I thanked Him for a faith that tells me that even though things like the World Trade Center attacks happen, somehow God can turn any situation around. My faith reminds me, as it states in David's Psalm 37:1, *"Fret not thyself because of evildoers."*

My faith tells me not to focus on the negative. True faith overcomes all fear. Indeed, I can board an airplane and fly without fear because I know that my destiny lies in Him. God is the master pilot, and I am safe in His arms. Even if the plane went down, I would still be safe in His arms because I have settled the "What should happen if I die" question. My faith teaches me that "to live is Christ, and to die is gain." This life is not all there is. We have an eternal home not made by hands.

I will not live in fear. I will not be blanketed in it to the point that my life is smothered out. My faith tells me that God is still in control! Faith causes us to dare to believe God...to trust Him...to rely on Him in the very face of fear. While thanking Him for favor, family, food, friends, and a sound frame of mind, I also thanked God for my faith. This faith teaches me that He is still in control of the universe and has not turned over the reigns of the world to evil.

The Apostle Paul's second letter to Timothy asserts, "For God hath not given us the spirit of fear; but of power, of love, and of a sound mind" (2 Tim. 1:7). Throughout the Scriptures, we see recurring themes where God's people walked by faith. It takes faith to walk with calm assurance, faith to stay in the right mind, and faith to keep your family together during trying times. Faith tells me that God will never leave nor forsake us. Even though we "walk through the valley and shadow of death," light still shines through the darkness. Hope still remains. Faith reminds us that our future is bright in Him.

For the Future...

The final thing for which I expressed gratitude was *for the future*. No matter what our circumstances may look like today, we *do* have a future.

What are you thankful for?
Encourage your family members to come to
the table with something special to thank
God for every day!

"For I know the plans I have for you,"
declares the LORD, "plans to prosper you
and not to harm you, plans to give you
hope and a future."
Jeremiah 29:11 (NIV)

Chapter Nine

Deliver Us From Evil

"*Our Father, which art in heaven, Hallowed be thy name. Thy kingdom come. Thy will be done in earth, as it is in heaven. Give us this day our daily bread. And forgive us our debts, as we forgive our debtors. And lead us not into temptation, but deliver us from evil...*" (Matt. 6:9-13).

The fact that Jesus shares the phrase, "deliver us from evil," in the prayer He taught His disciples, tells us that evil has longevity. Jesus would not give His disciples something to pray about that would be irrelevant later on. Everything Jesus taught them was not for them alone, but it was something also to be passed on to the next generation.

Jesus knew that evil would exist after He left the scene. Jesus knew that evil was going to be around, yet the good news is that we can be delivered from it.

Being delivered from something does not mean, however, that we will always avoid it. Sometimes it means that though we may be in the midst of it, God will open a door to take us *through* it. The word "evil" means something that causes pain. It is malignant. Jesus, however, equipped His people to handle every situation or crisis that could come upon us.

How can we be delivered from evil? Regardless of your personal definition of it, we have seen evil manifested in various forms. How can we be delivered in the midst of the evil? Three key words: "fear," "imitate," and "touch" will prove most helpful here. The acronym F-I-T, i.e., to be in a state of readiness and delivered from evil, is appropriate.

Fear

David, the Psalmist, declares in his 23rd psalm, *"I will fear no evil."* He did not declare that evil does not exist. He simply said, "I will not fear it." Jesus said in Matthew 15:19, *"For out of the heart proceedeth evil thoughts, murders, adulteries, fornications, thefts, false witness, blasphemies."* According to Jesus, seeds of evil find their origin in the human heart. Right now, even within us, there is a small seed of evil. That is why we need the Spirit of God to help us to fight against the lusts of the flesh. We are to abhor that which is evil and to cling to that which is good.

While our level of comfort has drastically changed

since September 11, we refuse to allow evil to paralyze our nation. Genuine faith causes us to maintain a steady resolve. Yes, "God is still our refuge and He remains our very present help in times of trouble."

"I will fear no evil! I will not be intimidated by evil!" These are emphatic statements that should reflect our values. Evil is real, but we can walk in faith and hope knowing that a caring and loving God is in charge.

Imitate

We are delivered from evil by not imitating it. Feelings of fear and anger are normal. We must, however, never allow fear and anger to engulf us with hate. Paul writes to the Romans in chapter 12 that we should not repay evil with evil, nor insult with insult. *"Vengeance is mine, sayeth the Lord."* In other words, ultimately, the Lord will handle our hurts and the evil things that rise up against us. Light will ultimately triumph over the darkness, and right will win over wrong. While it is normal to feel anger and fear, we cannot allow hate to overtake us because evil is always looking to control us!

Anyone who has seen "Star Wars" knows the character in black—Darth Vader. He was the one who tried to get Luke Skywalker to join the dark side. In one of those films, Darth Vader says, "Release your anger and join me." Evil is always looking for a convert.

A great man once said, "Let no man bring you so low as to hate him." When you are reduced to hate, it consumes you. Every waking moment becomes consumed with revenge. Indeed, we want justice to prevail, but revenge can grow like a cancer in the soul and mind. Why let your soul be consumed with hate? Make your mind up not to imitate evil.

Staying in Touch With God

We will fear no evil, and we will not imitate evil. What we will do, however, is to stay in touch with our God and walk close to Him. Life is so unpredictable. We should walk close enough to God that we gain strength from Him. As it is written in James 4:8, "Draw near to God, and He will draw near to you." The old saints in the African-American tradition would say, "I am sending up my timber every day." In essence, I am praying with consistency now because there may come a season where I am too overcome to pray later.

Several people have asked me, "Pastor, where was God on September 11, 2001? In response, I replied, "God who is sovereign, omniscient, and omnipresent was caring for us even during this great tragedy. On that Tuesday, God was in His position of Counselor and Comforter. God was both protecting and receiving His children. He was in the same place He was when Jesus, His own Son, was dying. God was in that plane appealing to a demented conscience and consoling innocent people. God was in the hospitals equipping medical personnel for something they never expected to see. God was equipping His people to minister to a world in chaos. So many more thousands of innocent lives could have been lost if the attack was just an hour later. God was right there all of the time. This is the only reason we are still here today.

Stay in touch with the God who still grieves. God grieves when our consciences are not moved, when our hearts remain unchanged, and when we are neglectful of our own families. All humanity is God's family. It is our responsibility to treat them as such.

Deliverance in the Midst of Evil

Evil will always be around, but Jesus teaches us to pray that He will, "Deliver us from evil." We can be delivered even while we are in the midst of it. Jesus Christ, the hope of the world, remains our comfort.

If our hearts and minds are void of the presence of God, we can have everything and be full of nothing at the same time. Far too many of us have our hands full, but our hearts are empty. Allow divine love to flow through your hearts right now. His peace and mercy are available to all who ask for it. Evil can bring people to God who have never drawn near to Him before. Tragedy has a way of reminding us of the issues that really matter.

Is there anyone you continue to hate?
Ask God to help you extend forgiveness to
them and to put them in God's hands.

---

*For what is a man profited, if he
shall gain the whole world, and lose his
own soul?*
Matthew 16:26

Chapter Ten

Carrying the Message

People of faith view the evening news differently than the rest of the world. Our perspective is deeply influenced by our understanding of biblical truth. As such, we raise our children as gifts from God and view our marriage vows as sacred covenants. My faith affects all of the decisions I make in life. Our faith should affect our job performance as well as our choice of employment.

The *U.S. News and World Report, Time Magazine,* and other media have reported how our country has been significantly affected since the World Trade Center attacks, especially the East Coast of the United States. One of the major problems in New York and New Jersey has been a sudden loss of jobs after the devastating effects of the terrorists' attacks on many areas of commerce.

With so many people looking for employment, a high level of anxiety appears to be present. If we walk in faith, however, we can walk in the promise that God will open the right doors for us and provide good jobs. Since work was instituted by God as recorded in Genesis 3:19, "By the sweat of your brow you will eat," He will provide a means of support for us. Sometimes one door is closed so that we are forced to pursue other options. When a new job proves elusive and cannot seem to be found, perhaps it is time to create your own job by starting your own business. Begin to use what has already been placed in your hands. Allow your faith to be stretched. Rest in the Lord and wait patiently for Him. Do not allow yourself to be caught up in the fears of the moment. God will not let you drown in the midst of adversity.

There are challenging days ahead. Multi-billion dollar corporations have been exposed for fraudulent activities and are now filing for bankruptcy. As a result, many people are being laid off and many others are left owning worthless stock. Some workers are now required to work longer and harder for the same pay. Life savings have vanished and middle-aged people are wondering how they will fund their retirement.

Without faith in God, we can be so depressed or embarrassed by our losses that we cannot even face our friends. Losing a home or a car does not mean that we have to lose our hope. Material possessions may make life more comfortable, but they do not define who we are as individuals. We were somebody special before we ever possessed anything of worth.

We are commanded to rise up and not remain depressed, overtaken, or overcome. We are called to be messengers of good news in these days and to bring tidings of comfort to our families, neighborhoods, and communities.

There will always be darkness to stand against while we are in this life. At one time, it covered the face of the earth, and it remains a reality. Even today, darkness presents itself through other people, cultures, and political systems. The good news, however, is that light cannot be overcome by the darkness. Regardless of how darkness is manifested or how powerful it may seem to be, if our lives are founded on faith, we will overcome the darkness in the end! Light will win out! God will take care of us!

This is the good news that we have in Him. It is the good news that should be overflowing from all people of faith. People should be able to find that good news when they come into the house of the Lord.

Our Responsibilities Now

What are our responsibilities now? Racial harmony is one area in which we can work to bring the message of good news to the world. Unfortunately, 9-11 did not solve the problems between the races. We are still very much divided and there is fear on both sides. For example, when was the last time we felt comfortable enough to invite someone of another race or culture to our homes for a meal?

If we are really going to live out the true meaning of the good news, we must progress beyond holding hands with those of another race or culture in a prayer meeting. We must venture out into the world and show people by our examples that we know how we are supposed to live. We must embody a translation of the biblical message for these contemporary times. Our lives must demonstrate the love that has been so freely given to us.

If I speak in the tongues of men and of angels, but have not love, I am only a resounding gong or a clanging cymbal. And now these three remain: faith, hope and love. But the greatest of these is love (1 Cor. 13:1,13 NIV).

How shall we live in this hour? How can we show the love of God? How can we, even in small ways, show more compassion, sensitivity, and understanding to one another? We can begin by being less arrogant and by greeting others as we pass by. We can begin by *looking up to* people, rather than *looking down at* them. Have you ever felt like you were looked down on? It is very hurtful.

How, then, should I translate the message of real love? Real biblical love—real Christianity—goes beyond singing songs and reading the Bible. It means translating the Bible into action. Our reaction to that statement might initially be to try and fulfill the Matthew 25 directive to feed the hungry and clothe the naked. Many of us want to feed the hungry or clothe the naked over in

61

Africa and in other areas, but when it comes to our own neighbors or communities, it is a different story. Maybe you have an old, senior citizen living on your street who does not have enough money to make ends meet after they pay their rent. How many senior citizens have gone into cardiac arrest because we did not take enough time to show compassion and shovel out their walkway?

We can show love and compassion in small and simple ways so that when others look on us, they will know that we are Christians by the love we demonstrate. When I was a boy in camp, there was one particular song that I remember, "They will know that we are Christians by our love..." Not by the noise we make in our meetings or by the size or beauty of our buildings. They will know that we are Christians by a love demonstrated by our actions, not just our words.

We must translate this message for this hour. Then we must transfer this message of love to the next generation. Sometimes this is difficult to do because so many of us have forgotten where we came from. We must always remember that it was someone else's prayers, hard work, and support that helped to make us who we are today.

I have a clergy robe that I pull out and wear in church services two or three times a year. It is full of meaning for me because my late father and my mother, who is now a member of the church where I pastor, bought it for me when I graduated from Princeton Seminary. This was the robe that I wore when I came to our church as a new pastor 19 years ago. It is symbolic of the sacrifices my parents made for me throughout the years. In return, I am making sacrifices for my children. Our responsibility as Christians is to bring the message of hope and to sacrifice for those who are to come after us. They will know we are Christians by our love. The character of love is this:

Love is not puffed up. Love does not behave rudely and it does not seek its own. It is not provoked easily and it thinks no evil. Love does not rejoice in iniquity but love rejoices in the truth. And love bears all things and believes all things and hopes all things and endures all things and love never fails. But whether there are prophecies, they will fail and whether there are tongues, they will cease, and whether there is knowledge, it will vanish away. For we know in part and we prophesy in part but when that which is perfect is come then that which is in part will be done away. When I was a child I spoke like a child, I understood like a child, I thought as a child, but when I became a man, I put away childish things. For now we see in the mirror dimly, but then face to face. Now I know in part, but then I shall know just as I also am known. And now abideth faith, hope, love, these three, but the greatest of these is love (1 Cor. 13).

Every one of us should strive to do our best to love others and, thereby, bring a taste of heaven to the earth. God has called us to change the world and we must do it by our love. We cannot exist as an island unto ourselves.

We all need each other and must learn to work, walk, and pray together as brothers and sisters in Christ.

Let love be our answer for hate. Let kindness be our answer for the terror others bring to us. Let love conquer the fear in which the terrorists would like to drown us. Our God is able!

How can you demonstrate your love
to your family, relatives, friends, co-workers,
neighbors, and even strangers?

This is how we know what love is:
Jesus Christ laid down his life for us.
And we ought to lay down our lives for
our brothers.
1 John 3:16 (NIV)

Chapter Eleven

What Do We Now Need?

If the truth were told, most of us probably have what we need. If we need anything at all, it is probably more of God and His influence over our lives. I need more love, patience, and understanding. I really do not need more money, another pair of shoes, another suit, or another car. What I do need, however, is more of God and His grace. What I need is a little more wisdom to know how to use my time and value those things that are of true value. What I need is for God to expand my territory to include someone who may not have a daddy anymore. I need to expand my territory to include the work of the kingdom of God, the mission of the gospel, and those who do not have daily bread. I need to remember those whose needs may only be met because I help meet them. God has provision for every one of our needs. He has also given many of us extra to help provide for someone else's necessity as well.

Some of us may be facing a cancer diagnosis or bankruptcy. Some of us may have just built homes and suddenly have no job. By faith, however, we declare, "Evidently, God you allowed this. I trust that You are going to show up. I am just going to trust that You are going to meet my needs." You will not drown in your disaster, you will not drown in your debt, and you will not drown in your disappointment.

We have all been disappointed at times. Perhaps you have tried to have a baby and could not. The marriage that you thought was going to be blissful, ended in divorce. You cannot believe your mate walked out on you. You cannot believe they fired you from that job to which you gave your entire life. You cannot believe your parents did not pour into you the way they should have.

Isaiah 43:2 states,

When you pass through the waters, I will be with you; and when you pass through the rivers, they will not sweep over you. When you walk through the fire, you will not be burned; the flames will not set you ablaze.

The psalmist says that we are hard pressed on every side. Everywhere we turn we can feel it, but God will not let it crush us. We may be perplexed, but should not be in despair. Even though we are persecuted and pierced on every side, we will never be forsaken. We may be struck down, but not destroyed because God has us in the grip of His mercy. We will not drown in fear and turmoil when we remind ourselves of His goodness and the care that He has for us every day.

Speaking the Right Words

We have to continually speak the right words in our spirits. The Bible says in Proverbs 18:21, *"Death and life are in the power of the tongue."* It does not matter what the x-ray shows, we will declare in faith God's perfect will for our lives. Our children will be saved, and we will be sanctified and whole in our minds and bodies. We must declare that we will prosper and be in health, even as our souls prosper. Confess to yourself: "I will not die young. I will not live in pain. I will not be bound by depression." Furthermore, in faith we have to declare victory over everything that involves us—our families, wives, husbands, children, and businesses. Let us declare that we still belong to God and will not be drowned by disaster, debt, or despair. We will not be drowned by disappointment or discouragement. We are His and He is ours. We must give ourselves to God in a fresh way.

One Christmas, my nieces gave me a calendar containing some of the famous quotes of Dr. Martin Luther King Jr.'s sermons. One quote states, "The belief that God will do everything for man is as unattainable as the belief that man can do everything for himself. It, too, is based on a lack of faith. We must learn that to expect God to do everything while we do nothing is not faith, but rather superstition."

The small trials that we think we go through are often not trials at all. I think September 11 taught us that lesson. It was then that some of us began to put our problems in their proper perspective. Many of us are spoiled, self-centered, and insensitive to the pain of others. If everything does not go our way, we feel like God has failed us. He has not failed us at all. We are just experiencing a season of challenge.

People are coming to the house of God these days, looking for some kind of word from the Lord. They are looking for an answer and peace in the midst of chaos. Oftentimes, before they give ear to a man or woman speaking from the pulpit, they are going to listen to your testimony. Let us take great care that our testimonies are full of hope, care, and concern. It always behooves us to say something nice, edifying, uplifting, and enriching to others. God does not prevent bad things from happening in the life of every believer. He does, however, fill us with comfort so that, in return, we can comfort others.

We need to make sure that we are working on our spiritual nature, creating a firm foundation. Recently, I had a little landscaping work done at the house. I like greenery and trees and, therefore, had one part of the yard done. When it was completed, the landscaper called and said, "Don, I would like to talk to you about the next phase." I asked him, "The next phase of what?" When he replied, "The yard," I said, "I do not care right now about the trees around the driveway or the shrubbery. I need landscaping done on my soul. I need God to do some landscaping in me." September 11 helped me to recognize that I needed wisdom to reprioritize some things in my life.

We may be in church every Sunday and read the Bible daily, but we still need some work done in our hearts. Too often, we are stingy, selfish, and gossip about one another. Too often, we are not committed or caring and, therefore, need God to work on us.

In Psalm 130, David wrote, "Out of the depths have I cried unto thee, O Lord." As I watched the twin towers come crashing down, something began to rise up in me that helped me more clearly understand what Jesus said to the rich man. "For what shall it profit a man, if he shall gain the whole world, and lose his own soul?" (Mr. 8:36).

Frances Stanton-Martinez was at the coffee machine in one of the Twin Towers when the plane hit. She went running out of the building and lived to share about it. She understands that verse differently now, too.

Charles Aniton is a young man who had planned to go into work first and then later to the gym. Something in his spirit told him to go to the gym first. As he was finishing his workout at 8:30 a.m., he was walking toward the World Trade Center and saw the plane hit the tower above him. By the mercy and grace of God, his life was spared. His testimony speaks clearly of his sense of divine protection over his life. (See Part II for their testimonies.)

Asking for God's Mercy

We need to pray for God's mercy for the nation and

His comfort for the thousands of those whose hearts are yet raw in grief. Even a year later, many are still shrouded by depression, grief, anxiety, and pain. While we comfort the bereaved, let us pause to give God praise for the safety of our own lives and those whose lives were spared.

The Lord is our strength, not our material possessions, careers, or lifestyle. All of those things were insignificant on September 11. What could people's money do for them on that Tuesday morning? Each of my family members carry a cellphone, but none of us could use them on that frightful day. We could only communicate in the spirit. I prayed, "Lord, touch my child in college, cover my baby in school, and cover my daughter in high school. Please remember each of the saints, God."

Learning the Language of Faith

We have to learn the language of faith and make sure that we have faith to draw on when trouble comes. In all honesty, I was so shocked and traumatized that day that I could hardly find the words to pray. While I knew the Holy Ghost was making intercession for me, I also knew that I could draw on the prayers that I had already prayed when things were going well. I have a reserve of faith. I do not just try to dig deep when trouble comes. I keep my lamp trimmed and burning throughout each day. I live this life as if today might be my last. I stay in communication with God because we do not know when trouble will come. The psalmist says in Psalm 46, "God is our refuge and strength...a very present help in trouble."

Release Our Fears

How do we cope with fear? We must release our fears and let God handle them. God has a word for our nation. In the midst of the chaos and calamity, our word of comfort is that Christ is still the answer. Christ is still our hope and our Lord.

Although not everyone believes as we do, we still must walk side-by-side with all humanity and live in mutual respect. This is a nation with many different cultures, creeds, and streams of thought. Yet, humanity is under God's created order, and He loves all of us.

Ultimately, I believe that God is trying to tell us to live our lives in a state of readiness. Unfortunately, September 11 has caused many people to fall into fear when God desires to bring us into a new place of readiness and repentance.

September 11 brought us together in a unique way. For a short time, we all experienced, to some degree, the reality of being like one, big family. God, somehow, used this horrific tragedy to refocus our priorities. Sometimes God uses tragedy to help us understand what is really important in life. We need to make that principle a permanent part of us.

We must be sure that we are anchored, not in those things that moths and dust can corrupt, but rather, firmly grounded in what is incorruptible and eternal. We are connected to another world...to a city called heaven.

Spend some time thinking about what fears you have and then give them to the Lord. Ask Him to help you trust Him with them.

Trust in the LORD with all your heart and lean not on your own understanding; in all your ways acknowledge him, and he will make your paths straight. Do not be wise in your own eyes; fear the LORD and shun evil. This will bring health to your body and
nourishment to your bones.

Chapter Twelve

Faith in the Face of Fear

I t is difficult for us to remember, particularly in times like these, that God is still our refuge. Even now, the Lord remains our light and our salvation. We have no need to fear.

In times like these, we need a sure footing and a firm foundation to stand as a tower against the onslaught of fear. What is the result of fear? When fear grips us, we become paralyzed. Have you ever gone to the doctor for some tests and lived for several days in complete fear because of the "what ifs?" We cannot allow ourselves to become gripped by fear because fear will leave us immobilized.

I am challenged by Psalm 37:1-2,

Fret not thyself because of evildoers, neither be thou envious against the workers of iniquity. For they shall soon be cut down like the grass, and wither as the green herb.

Now, this is a real challenge, particularly when we are overexposed to iniquity and the works of evil. We must make a deliberate effort to guard our minds and spirits against negativity in these times. Overexposure to bad news on television, in newspapers, and at the office is not healthy. Such saturation can leave us extremely pessimistic. We need faith, hope, and optimism in these days. We must focus on our help, which comes from God, not on our hurts. Fear does not come from God. The Apostle Paul exhorts his son in the ministry, Timothy, with this faith-building admonition:

For God hath not given us the spirit of fear; but of power, and of love, and of a sound mind (2 Tim. 1:7).

The choice must be made to walk in faith. There are times in my life when I have felt as if I was in the crucible of pressure. One thing after another crowded my mind and sometimes challenged my peace. While the stresses of life can cause anxiety and panic, they are not coming from God. God does not give us a spirit of fear, panic, or dread. Much of what we obsess over and worry about never happens. Walk by faith. The Lord is with you!

Worry Does Not Add to Character

The Master, while speaking with His disciples, warned them against worry:

And why take ye thought for raiment? Consider the lilies of the field, how they grow; they toil not, neither do they spin. Therefore take no thought, saying, What shall we eat? or, What shall we drink? or, Wherewithal shall we be clothed? (Matt. 6:28, 31).

Worry will not add anything to your life or your character. Suffering changes us, but worry drains us. These are days of heightened anxiety. Many of us feel a little more anxious. We have to work at walking in peace.

Psalm 37 gives us some positive direction:

Trust in the Lord and do good, dwell in the land and feed on his faithfulness. Delight yourself also in the Lord and he shall give you the desires of your heart. Commit your way to the Lord, trust also in Him and he shall bring it to pass. He shall bring forth your righteousness as the light and your justice as the noonday.

The psalmist exhorts us to wait patiently for God. Do not fret because of those who prosper in their ways, or because of the one who brings wicked schemes to pass. We must cease from anger and not fret, because it only causes us harm.

For the LORD loveth judgment, and forsaketh not his saints; they are preserved for ever: but the seed of the wicked shall be cut off. The righteous shall inherit the land, and dwell therein for ever (Psalm 37:28-29).

We serve a God who will speak to us in the midst of this horrific display of terrorism through His Word. We know that the wicked may get by temporarily, but they will ultimately not prosper. The psalmist tells us to shift our focus from what the wicked are doing, and put it on God and His faithfulness. Trust Him to bring us through our calamities and great disappointments. Biblical faith stands against evil with steady resolve. It looks tragedy square in the eye and declares, "Even though they slay me, yet will I trust in Him" (Job 13:15). Even in the midst of darkness, I will fear no evil.

But now thus saith the LORD that created thee, O Jacob, and he that formed thee, O Israel, Fear not: for I have redeemed thee, I have called thee by thy name; thou art mine. When thou passest through the waters, I will be with thee; and through the rivers, they shall not overflow thee: when thou walkest through the fire, thou shalt not be burned; neither shall the flame kindle upon thee. For I am the LORD thy God, the Holy One of Israel, thy Saviour: I gave Egypt for thy ransom, Ethiopia and Seba for thee. (Is. 43:1-3).

We will always belong to the Lord and, therefore, we

shall not drown in the raging waters. When we pass through the waters, He will be with us. Through the rivers, they shall not overflow us. When we walk through the fire, we will not be burned. Why? Because we are the Lord's! My friends, this is our faith...this is our hope.

God's Glory Seen in Us

Arise, shine for your light has come and the glory of the Lord is risen upon you. For behold the darkness shall cover the earth and deep darkness the people. For the Lord will arise over you and his glory will be seen upon you.(Is. 60:1-2).

In these days of great challenge, allow God's glory to be seen in and through you. We, who know the Lord as our eternal hope, are determined to walk by faith. Walking by faith before September 11, 2001 meant an entirely different thing than walking by faith since then. After September 11, the world, as we knew it, changed. Walking by faith now means that even when I walk outside in the parking lot and open up my mail, or when I board an airplane or enter a crowded building, I do it in faith.

If we are not careful, our minds can go a thousand different ways, and we can find ourselves feeding on negativity and fear.

With what are we feeding our psyches and our spirits? We need the confidence and strength that can be found in the Holy Scriptures. A daily devotional life, filled with prayer, will ground us in faith.

He that dwelleth in the secret place of the most High shall abide under the shadow of the Almighty (Ps 91:1).

There is, indeed, a place in God that is safe and secure from the storms of this life. In this, we find comfort.

On that September morning, we witnessed a dastardly attack on our nation of horrific proportion. It was a tragedy beyond words. At the same time, we saw humanity come together as family. Together we prayed, cried, joined in the rescue and recover effort, donated money, food, and blood. Together, as a family, we bled. Our hearts bled for those we knew, loved, and lost.

On that September morning, the rich died with the poor, the black died with the white, and the red died with the yellow. White collar workers died alongside the blue collar workers; the educated died with the illiterate. We all bleed, and in time, we will all heal. Together, we are rebuilding the torn ruins in New York and Washington, D.C. Together, we are helping families put children, who lost parents on that day, through college. Together, we are serving in the armed services. Together, we are calling on the God whose watchful eye supports and sustains us. This is our faith! This is our hope!

The words of the old African-American spiritual ring ever true, especially now...

If I can help somebody as I pass along,
If I can spread love's message to a world once wrong.
If I can show some traveler that he's traveling wrong,

Then my living will not be in vain.
My living will not be in vain.

May it be said of us, as it was said of the early church, "They too turned the world upside down." When we get to heaven, we will be at home. This is not our home. We have a home and we have a city not made with hands, which is eternal in the heavens.

"Let not your heart be troubled, you believe in God, believe also in me. In my Father's house are many mansions and I go there to prepare a place for you." Amen.

Faith is what we need when we walk in the face of overwhelming fear. Faith will give us new vision and purpose. This faith declares that we will not only survive, but we will indeed thrive! We must declare,

"FAITH IN THE FACE OF FEAR!"

PART II

TESTIMONIES OF PEOPLE INVOLVED IN THE TRAGEDY OF 9-11

Chapter Thirteen

Testimonies

O n the eleventh day of the ninth month in the year 2001 at 8:48 a.m., hi-jacked jetliners filled with terror-stricken passengers became instruments of death for untold thousands and the destruction of two of America's symbols of strength—the World Trade Center in New York City and the Pentagon in Washington D.C.

We call 911 in case of emergencies, and this was indeed an American emergency. This was, in fact, an emergency of emergencies. More than 100 firefighters, police, and emergency personnel were lost in the collapses of the twin towers while trying to figure out how to rescue people stranded many stories above Manhattan streets. Others at the Pentagon lost their lives, too, when a portion of the structure was totally destroyed. A news commentator reported that even the 911 operators needed special counseling given the frequency and graphic nature of the calls on that day.

Our nation was still in shock weeks afterward. I have witnessed the blank looks, grief and anger on people's faces. On the night after the attack, I asked my wife how she felt and she said she was "depressed." Let me say to you that salty, bitter tears have run down my face more than once as I have tried to process this senseless tragedy.

Psychologists are saying that we are collectively struggling with these events, and they describe the struggle, along with its range of sentiments, as post-traumatic stress syndrome. The reality of the loss of loved ones, the loss of symbols, the loss of property, the loss of our sense of safety, and the loss of self-confidence have left us with a glaring sense of vulnerability and pain.

Today, almost one year later, our nation is wondering if there is an answer. Is there a word from the Lord? Jesus said, "Blessed are they who mourn." We are in mourning and our nation is grieving. Interestingly enough, the Master also said, "Happy are they who grieve." To "mourn" is to speak of a grief that takes hold of a person and cannot be hidden. It is a sorrow that causes the heart to ache. It is a sorrow that brings uncontrollable tears to the eyes. To mourn is to process one's pain. It is to express and deal with the hurt that you feel inside.

Blessed is the one who has endured the ugliest sorrow and the most incredible pain that life can bring. The Arabs have a proverb: All sunshine makes a desert. In other words, the land on which the sun shines continually will soon become a parched place in which no fruit will grow. There are certain things that only the rain will produce and certain experiences that only sorrow will bring about. Yes, sorrow can show us things about ourselves that pleasant times could never reveal.

Robert Browning Hamilton's poem, "Along the Road," captured this thought when he wrote: "I walked a mile with pleasure, she chattered all the way, but she left me none the wiser. I walked a mile with sorrow, and never a word she said. But oh, the things I learned from her, when sorrow walked with me along the road."

It is no secret that New York is a city that promotes power, influence, money, and education. One's social status is of great importance in the Big Apple. A member of our congregation, Sister Sonja Tolbert, was in New York City during the catastrophe. She related that during the frantic efforts to escape the mayhem of crashing planes and collapsing buildings, nobody looked at what anybody was wearing. Nobody cared about race, color, creed or whether you were literate or illiterate. It did not matter whether you lived uptown or downtown or whether your residence was in a brownstone or a homeless shelter. Everyone was engaged in a passionate effort to help everyone else to safety. The common tragedy had woven all of them together, despite their differences, into one people. This is a lesson of comfort that is often obscured in pleasant times but made clear in periods of tragedy and sorrow. Jesus said, "Blessed are those who mourn for they shall be comforted." He will comfort you!

What shall we do in the wake of this colossal tragedy? People gathered into religious institutions across America for answers, and words of encouragement that might help them through their tumultuous time, and rightfully so. For David said, "Some trust in chariots and some in horses, but we will trust, we will remember the name of the Lord our God." While we appreciate Wall Street and the stock market, while we are grateful for the Central Intelligence Agency and our sophisticated weaponry, our ultimate trust must be in the Lord our God.

Let me ask a question. What do you do when you call 911 and the recording says all circuits are busy? Who do you call when the lines are jammed and the operator says, "Please try your call again?" I suggest that you dial a little higher. Rather than dialing 911, we must dial 111: one for the Father, one for the Son, and one for the Holy Spirit. The old saints of my youth used to sing, "Call Him up, call Him up, His line is never busy, tell Him what you want. Jesus is on the main line now."

At the close of the day, our salvation and preservation will not be found in our economic strength, nor will it be found in our military might. In the end, our hope is in the name of the Lord, our God. The hymn is more than 160 years old, but Edward Mote's poetic words still ring relevant.

"My hope is built on nothing less than Jesus' blood and righteousness. I dare not trust the sweetest frame but wholly lean on Jesus name. On Christ, the Solid Rock I stand all other ground is sinking sand; all other ground is sinking sand."

Those Who Were Spared

As a pastor, I have seen the lives of many of my congregation affected by tragedy. I want to share with you accounts from some of them who were in or near the World Trade Center when the tragedy happened and who thankfully survived.

Charles Aniton, a bus driver and a member of our congregation, shares his personal account of that tragic day.

"September 11th began as a normal day for me as a bus driver. While enroute to New York City, I was driving on the New Jersey Turnpike, just passing beside Newark Airport, when I heard a still small voice in my spirit that said, 'DON'T GO!' Not paying much attention, I passed the thought out of my mind. As I was dropping off passengers in the Wall Street area, I heard that same voice again, and it said, 'DON'T GO!' but this time I felt a greater urgency in my spirit. Still not comprehending what the urgent feeling of warning was, I dismissed it once again.

"After parking my bus on Pier 40 at West Houston and West Street, I changed out of my uniform and into my street clothes, preparing to go to my doctor's appointment just two blocks from the World Trade Center. To get to my appointment, I needed to take the subway train to the World Trade Center. As I was walking to the subway with a co-worker, just as I reached the subway entrance, suddenly I heard the voice again. This time the voice said, 'DON'T GO! DON'T TAKE THE TRAIN!' The feeling of warning was so strong that I changed my mind and went around the corner to the gym to work out. I still had no clue what the warning was about. I now questioned the Lord and said, 'Lord Jesus, what is going on? You know that I have a nine o'clock doctor's appointment,' but there was no answer from the Lord.

"Twenty minutes later, I heard sirens coming from every direction and all headed the same way—toward the Trade Center. Someone who was in the weight room with me said, 'It must be a very bad fire,' and I replied, 'I do not think so.' The last time I had heard similar sirens was when someone had bombed the World Trade Center. Suddenly someone else burst into the room and said that a plane had just hit the World Trade Center. At that moment I started thanking the Lord and praising Him for sparing my life, because I would have come out of the subway into the World Trade Center at the same time that the plane hit.

"I left the gym immediately and reached West Street where I had a view of the Trade Center. I had just missed seeing the second plane hitting the World Trade Center. It was total bedlam, and people were running all over the place. I stood there praying for the people who I knew were dead on those floors that were hit by the planes. Then suddenly, in my spirit, I felt an urgency to pray for people's souls, praying that they would receive the Lord as Savior. Then without warning, the first tower started to collapse before my eyes. The sound of the roar was so loud and the sight was so awful and frightening, that I still today have visions of the Trade Center coming down. It is a day in my life that I still relive in my mind."

Frances Stanton-Martinez, a member of the church for many years and is employed by Merrill Lynch, shares her story.

"My day began with my usual rush to make the 6:57 a.m. train from Hamilton Station. I did one of two things during my commute to the World Financial Center, which could last anywhere from 1-1/2 to 1-3/4 hours. Contemplating whether to listen to the local Christian radio station or continue to read *The Prayer of Jabez*, I opted to listen to the radio and just relax until I arrived at Newark Penn Station where the Path Train connected for my ride to the World Trade Center.

"Along with the thousands of other New Jersey commuters during rush hour, I boarded the Path in the hope of finding a seat. The day seemed unusually warm as the sun beamed through the train windows. Making my normal stop by the ladies' room to check my make-up and fix the dishevelment from the the commute, I greeted the other women in the bathroom and the attendant who was always cleaning there.

"I rode up the escalator to the Mall Level under One World Trade Center, passed by the pharmacy, dodged other commuters rushing to work and went up the next level of escalators to the street level. Once there, I walked across the side of the court area, which was a gathering point for lunch or coffee breaks during the workday. There were tables outside with umbrellas and stoops where people sat by the monuments, a central waterfall, and street vendors who sold their wares. The central hub also served to join the Trade Center buildings, World Financial buildings, and hotels to create what seemed to be a capsule, housing and servicing the professional elite of New York.

"I passed by the security station of the U.S. Customs Office and continued through the glass turnstiles entering the crosswalk leading to the World Financial Center. I glanced up at the monitor mounted in the ceiling at the entrance to note the time, which was 8:36 a.m. Continuing down the corridor of the crosswalk, I went through another set of glass turnstiles entering the Winter Gardens, which was the entrance to the World Financial Center. The Winter Gardens were breathtaking. There were many restaurants and shops below. Greenery hung from the ceiling and music always played as the people went to their offices. Outside of the palladium, you could see the New Jersey side of the river and to the left, the Statue of Liberty.

"I went through the check points, gaining access to One World Financial Center (the South tower) with my Merrill Lynch employee identification, greeted the security personnel and continued to the elevator designated for floors 35 and above. I got off at the 39th floor and went through the glass doors to my workstation where my boss was already viewing equities and market fluctuations. From his office, you could see the Statue of Liberty and the many boats in the harbor, not to mention the beautiful view of the New Jersey coastline.

"Having not yet changed from my commuter shoes to office heels, I put down my travel gear to retrieve money from my purse for coffee and oatmeal from the cafeteria, which was my usual routine for the morning. The other workers in the area were settling in for the activity that commenced with the bell that signaled the beginning of the trading day on Wall Street.

"All of a sudden, a woman began yelling frantically, 'Get out of the building! Move, move, get out of the building!' I looked up to see everyone scampering for exit doors and stairwells. I, too, began to run to the end of the aisle that I had just walked up. Not knowing what had happened, people had begun to run back to their workstations in total confusion and panic. Fire drills were held occasionally, but no one ever really paid attention to them. I wondered if this was one of them. My boss asked me what was happening and I said, 'We have to get out of the building!" He ran in front of me and another man who worked in my group followed me trying to exit the building as instructed. I remember now that as we entered the stairwell and started down the stairs the same woman who sounded the emergency yelled to us that the stairwell did not end at the street, but ended at a door that was locked about eight flights down. After the men attempted to open the door for what seemed an eternity, we ran back up the stairs to the 39th floor to gain access to another exit. When we opened the door of that stairwell, other people fleeing the building from the floors above met us. We entered the flow of traffic and kept running down the stairs as fast as we could. Questions were asked as the people kept running down the stairs, not yet knowing exactly why we had to evacuate the building. I just kept running and realized the length of my dress was hindering my speed, so I lifted the hemline and kept going. The stairs never seemed to end. My mind went to my husband who was constantly reminding me to go to the gym and work out. At that moment, I was thankful to God for his insisting that I keep in shape and was able to run without being overly winded. The flow began to slow down as more people were entering the stairwell, and people began to tire and stop running. People began to cry, scream and pant from exhaustion and fear. Some people did decide to stop and rest. I kept running with the prayer that we would reach the end soon. Once we reached the bottom of the stairs, we hurried down a long corridor under the World Financial Center and, at the end, we were met by someone who yelled for us to keep moving. Feeling some sense of relief, my two co-workers and I kept up a quick pace exiting the building.

"In front of the exit doors was One World Trade Center (the North tower). I ran out of the building into the midst of the emergency. I first ran to the left, but debris was falling from the sky, smoke was bellowing, and fire was roaring from the building directly across the street. People were standing there in amazement, pointing to the building in disbelief. I continued to quickly walk under the crosswalk and saw the people standing under it, thinking they should not be there. The World Trade Center already seemed to look like it was tilting. Fire engines were racing down the street, and police cars were everywhere. People were crying hysterically. I then realized I was alone. I looked around not knowing where to go or what to do. All emergency workers were dealing with the event at hand. I had left my belongings on the 39th floor. I thought at first I would just stand to the side, out of the way, but what I now know to be the guidance of the Holy Ghost, told me to keep walking away from the buildings.

"Looking at the billowing smoke, and the roaring flames, and hearing the screams of the people, I noticed a woman above the fire floor waving a white towel in the hope that someone could help her. I then noticed people jumping out of the windows and falling so quickly, and yet, it was like they were in slow motion with their arms waving. A man and a woman jumped out together holding hands. Debris was falling with them so it was, at times, hard to detect if what was falling was people or debris. I kept walking, trying to figure out what I was going to do and if I was far enough out of harm's way. I stopped by the fence, put my head against it, and began to beg God for help. I was about two blocks away, but the burning building was still so close to me.

"Rumors began to fly as people who felt a safe distance away began to talk, trying to determine what had actually happened. Some said it was a bomb like before. One lady said a plane flew into the building accidentally. Trying hard to comprehend that fact, I said, 'If a plane hit the building, where are its remains? There has to be something in the street or somewhere. There's nothing.' She agreed and at that very moment, the second plane flew into Two World Trade Center and burst into flames.

"People again panicked and began running as fast as they could, and I was among them. I ran down the street about one block and ran another block to an open deserted lot. There was a bench there, so I sat down and tried to comprehend what had happened. I looked down to find out what I was clutching in my hand and remembered that I was able to get a dollar and some change out of my purse before I began running. How was I going to get home? How was I going to reach anyone?

"People were running past me. There were others who were trying to use their cell phones, but were told that none of them were working. I must have been there for a while, but everything was happening so fast. I looked up and both buildings were now uncontrollably on fire . There was nothing anyone could do. We were all so helpless. I walked back up the street in the direction I had come from in the hope that an emergency worker could tell me what to do.

"I reached the paved street in view of Two World Trade Center, and it was at that point that the building collapsed. There was a loud sound like a train and people again began to run away. People were crying and screaming, 'We are going to die!' Children clutched their parents who, I am sure, were wondering what was happening and at the same time trying not to traumatize them. Fire engines sped down the street; cars were abandoned. A woman was asking for assistance to calm her down; she was shaking uncontrollably. I grabbed her by the shoulders and shook her to repeat what I heard in my mind. 'Keep walking!' Another woman who had stopped with those she was running with became hysterical. She began to scream, yelling, 'What is wrong with you people? You are standing here watching people die! They are jumping out of the windows to their deaths. Are you enjoying this? How can you just stand here? Are you not human?' A man she was with grabbed her and held her, and she began to break down hysterically.

I turned my face to the cement building and began to cry. I had to keep my composure. I had no time to lose. I had to keep running or I, too, could be a casualty. By this time, emergency personnel were on the side streets working crowd control. They instructed everyone to walk down toward the harbor staying away from the tall buildings.

"As we rushed along the boardwalk by the harbor, people from the nearby streets were converging into one area. After a while, it was hard to walk, let alone run if we had to. You had to go with the flow of the crowd, whichever way it went. We came to an area on the boardwalk where it turned a corner and continued up the river. Once I reached the bottleneck, a plane was sighted over us and people began to scream again after making a mental connection with the two planes that had just flown into the World Trade Center buildings. The crowd began to push through an aluminum fence. People began to fall, scream, and cry. An emergency worker looked up also in fear but determined that it was an American jet. He screamed immediately, 'It is one of ours!'

"One of ours? Why did we need jets flying over New York? I remember thinking. What was happening? I finally got past the aluminum fence and began to run with the other people. I remember thinking, 'Lord, I know you do not mean for me to die like this. This cannot be Your will. Or is it? If it is, I commit myself to Your care.' I was about to lose it again but had to talk myself back to composure.

"By this time, the crowd control team was asking

people to be careful and just walk as quickly as we could. Of course, this did no good because people were scared to death and confused. There was a man who was walking with a crowd that said, 'The Pentagon has just been bombed!' I stopped dead in my stride and repeated what I knew had to be a mistake. 'The Pentagon?' This man looked me directly in the eye and repeated most emphatically, 'Yes, the Pentagon!' I then realized we were being attacked. The realization hit me like a ton of bricks, and I began to feel my insides sink. I could not move for a brief while.

"I left the boardwalk because it had temporarily ended and began to walk in the street. I could not believe this was happening and I kept looking back. I continued to walk but it felt as if I was in a dream and would soon wake up safely. I kept looking back at the remaining building that was burning. Sometimes I was walking fast, sometimes running, and sometimes hardly moving in disbelief. All of a sudden, there was a thundering so loud and intense that the ground shook. I turned around and saw that the building was crumbling. It was like a loud train, and it fell in what seemed to be slow motion. A cloud of smoke began to rush down the street, and again I found myself literally running for my life. The cloud seemed to be coming closer and closer, but I just kept running. People were screaming and running. Children were being dragged by their parents. Emergency vehicles were speeding down the street. Emergency workers were running. There was a strong smell in the air. 'Keep running, keep running!' That's all I could think. The cloud stopped, but I was not far enough yet.

"I went over by the harbor railing. There was an elderly man leaning over the harbor railing, weeping from his heart. He said he remembered when those buildings were built, and they were beautiful. He said, 'What is happening? Has the world gone mad? I've never experienced anything like this, even in the war. What am I going to do?' I looked him in the eye and again repeated what I heard inside of me. 'Keep walking. You'll be all right.' I walked further and then decided to rest. People were lined up at the pay phones, so I could forget trying to reach anyone that way. The cell phones still were not working because people everywhere were unsuccessfully trying to use them.

"I began to walk again and noticed a professionally dressed Latino woman who seemed to be able to use her phone. She had made contact with her brother in Boston. Her brother had told her that all planes had been grounded. I asked if she could make a call for me. She explained that she did not know how long the signal would last, but if I gave her the number I wanted to call and her brother in Boston would make contact. I gave her the number to my father's telephone. People began to see we were getting through, and they began also to ask for help. She lost the signal after getting my number through and attempting to help two other people. I just stood there, and I guess she could see the desperation on my face. She asked if I was all right. I guess at that point, I broke into what must have seemed like multitudes of sentences describing my circumstances. She invited me to walk with her for help.

"As we talked, I learned that she had a brother who

worked at the Pentagon and that she was concerned for his life. Her calls to Boston were to her other brother who was going to continue the search for him. Her cell phone rang and it was her brother in Boston who said that her other brother was held up in a bunker in Washington and was fine. He also said the entire East Coast was under jet patrol and was shooting down anything flying because all planes were grounded.

"We continued to walk after she lost the signal. We found that we both had thought of the same plan if another plane was going to run into a building. We were going to jump in the water. We passed a stand that was selling water and she asked if I wanted bottled water. I said no, but she bought it anyway because I needed it. We kept walking until it must have been about 3:00 p.m. I remember thinking that it seemed like only a while ago that l was going to get coffee. She said her feet hurt, and she needed a cigarette, so we stopped to rest so she could smoke. I asked to use her cell phone. Who could I call that would be sure to be home? I could not chance calling my husband's cell phone because he was working and always left it in his truck. No one would know I was all right until after he got off from work. I called my father. He answered the phone and I was so glad I made contact with someone. He heard my voice and said, "Thank God!' I could tell he was worried sick. I assured him I was all right and that I was going to try to get to a place of safety. Once I got there, I would try again to contact him. He said he would call everyone to let them know he had heard from me.

"I learned that the person's name, whom God had

sent to help me, was Eva from DeLoitte and Touche, and she actually worked in the World Trade Center. We kept walking and then she said, 'Let's cross the street.' 'Wait a minute,' I asked her, 'I thought you said you were going to stay by the water. Why have you now decided to head into the city?' She had a palm pilot and e-mailed her friend to ask if we could go there. Of course, she had agreed.

"We walked about another ten blocks to a loft where her friend happened to be an executive partner for Deloitte and Touche. They opened their home to us and served us food and beverages. They then said to prepare to settle in because troops may be called into the city, and all the trains and bridges had been closed. No one was leaving. I called my family and told them that I was safe and gave them the number where I could be reached. I then called my husband on the cell phone and found that he had left work in an attempt to find me. He offered to come for me, but I told him that there was no way he could get to me. All bridges and tunnels were closed. I would have to settle in where I was and leave in the morning if I could. About one hour later, I got a call from my sister in Virginia, who apologized for calling the house, but said she just had to hear my voice to be sure I was safe.

"Eva and her business partner began to call everyone they knew from work to see if they made it out of the building safely. Other people who had been caught up in the tragedy began to pour into the house. I sat on the couch watching the news so I could keep abreast of what was happening.

"I wanted to get out of New York in the worst way. I did not want to be caught up in the next day's events. I kept watching television. Finally, they announced that the trains were once again running. Now, I had to find a way to get to Penn Station. Not knowing anything about where I was, I asked how far away Penn Station was. One of the maids said that it was a good walk, but I could do it. Eva advised against it because she was concerned about looters and others taking advantage of what had occurred during the day, but the more I sat there the more I wanted to get safely home to New Jersey.

"Eva wanted another cigarette, so I went down to the street with her after having discussed with all the women in the house as to whether or not I should attempt to travel home. Once I was on the street, we walked to the subway to find that they had opened the E Train to Penn Station. We walked to the next subway to the E train, and I made up my mind that I was going to try to get home. Eva looked at me with great concern, but I was determined and so she did not try to convince me any more. She swiped me through the turnstile to the train, and I asked a worker the way to get to Penn Station. He told me and I looked back at Eva and the rest of the women to say goodbye. I was nervous because I had never been on a New York subway before, and it was one o'clock in the morning. When I arrived at Penn Station, I learned that they had suspended all fares so that people could ride free.

"I got on the train to Trenton. There was already a small group on it. There were people on the train who were intoxicated in an attempt to erase the trauma of the day. Others were asleep and others were still in a fog. There was a man on the train who had a cell phone, and I asked him if I could borrow it briefly to call my husband to let him know I was on my way home. I successfully reached him, and he met me at the train station to bring me safely home.

"The next day I could not walk from all the running I had done the day before. As I watched television, I saw that Merrill Lynch had set up an emergency number that they asked all employees to call to account for everyone. I called the number and became part of the count of those who survived.

"Needless to say, I will never forget September 11, 2001 and I must note that as I sat down to write this, I realized that I had worn all black to work on that day."

Deacon Cynthia Armour

"As a Port Authority employee of 18 years, I normally worked on the 68th floor in One World Trade Center with a normal arrival time of 8:00 a.m. On September 11, 2001, however, I was en route to Riviera Beach, on Continental Airlines. I am the oldest niece in my family, and my aunt's funeral was planned for September 12. Normally, I would not have been able to attend, but a good friend of mine insisted that I go and even purchased my ticket for me.

"While en route to Florida, the Captain made an announcement that there had been a catastrophe on the East Coast and that we would need to land at the nearest airport, which was Fort Lauderdale Airport. Once we landed and everyone's curiosity was piqued, people began making phone calls on cell phones. Mine, however, would not work. Prior to the announcement, I had been talking with the woman sitting next to me and had told her that I worked at the World Trade Center and had taken off to attend my aunt's funeral. Just then, she got through on her cell phone and told us that the World Trade Center buildings had collapsed and that there had been no survivors. I did not believe that could be possible and started calling on the name of Jesus. As we left the plane, other people were on their phones, so I proceeded to a nearby television just in time to see the second building go down.

"A very strange and frightening feeling came over me, and I immediately began to cry. I had a feeling of the rapture and of being left behind for a brief moment. I still could not believe my eyes and continued to cry and call on the name of Jesus, recalling all the people I had worked with for so many years and wondering where they were.

"Suddenly, I realized that I was stranded in an airport and unable to contact my dad who was probably thinking I was in the building. Then I remembered that I had told my aunts of my intention of attending the funeral, so they would be able to inform my dad that I was not in the building.

"After my tears stopped, the Lord sent me an angel. Another passenger, who was retired, insisted that I come with her, since we both had another 280 miles to go. Our only way out would be by a taxi. Not only had I been deserted by Jesus (or so I thought), but by the airline as well. After a 280-mile taxi ride with seven other passengers, talking to my Dad, and hearing there were some survivors from a resigned co-worker, I started to feel a little better. I also began to feel truly guilty, and asked God, "Lord why did you spare me?"

"My plans had involved my being in Florida for one day, but not a week. I was blessed that I was able to spend time with my surviving aunts and uncles in Florida. Upon talking with me, my aunt's pastor, who also knew Bishop Hilliard, said that the Lord sacrificed my aunt to bring me to Florida so that *I could live.*"

Charles Robbins

"The date of September 11, 2001 will remain with me, in all likelihood, for the rest of my life. It will stand out in a similar fashion to the date of November 22, 1963, the day that I turned 17 years old, and John F. Kennedy was assassinated. On the day that Kennedy was killed, I can remember, as can many others of my generation, exactly where I was and what I was doing.

"I was standing at my gym locker in high school when the principal initially indicated that the president was shot. At the time, the principal did not know that Kennedy was dead and a second announcement came shortly afterwards that he was in fact dead.

"I started working in New York City on June 1, 1999. This was the first time that I had held a position in New York and I found it to be quite a challenge, primarily because of the transportation issues of getting back and forth to my home in West Orange.

"Driving into New York on a regular basis was not an option for me, so I found myself experimenting with several routes into the city such as using the bus to the Port Authority and then catching trains downtown to my office near the World Trade Center. Eventually, I settled on a route that would have me drive into Newark and then catch the train to the World Trade Center. My office was located only a few blocks from the World Trade Center, and it is actually a pleasant walk most days after leaving the train.

"During August 2001, I experienced some severe pain in my knee, which I ultimately found to be a torn cartilage and arthritis. Since the damage was in my left leg, I was still able to drive. I decided to go to work, thinking that I would be able to pick up crutches on my way into the office, but as it turned out, there was no place to pick them up, so I limped into New York in great pain. Part of my route, of course, was going from the Path Train and upstairs to the street outside the World Trade Center to get to my office.

"When I got into the office, a co-worker could tell that I had been through a struggle getting in and encouraged me to get back home as soon as possible. The nurse was able to provide me with crutches and my boss insisted that I use a car service to get back to my car in Newark. I mention this to show how the Lord was looking out for me. If I had come through the World Trade Center in the shape that I was in on the day of the attack, I would not have been able to move quickly enough to get out of the building.

"On September 11, I was sitting at my desk when the first plane hit the World Trade Center. One of my co-workers said there was a plane crash, but I assumed it was a small plane that had lost altitude and there was probably "minimal" damage. Minutes later when the second plane hit, I knew it was no accident, but that something intentional had happened.

"I saw the police cars speeding to the scene immediately after the first plane hit and my co-worker had a picture from the internet showing what had happened from the first plane. It was surreal.

"When the second plane hit, I saw the flash from the explosion and what had been a crystal clear day turned suddenly into darkness. Smoke filled the sky and papers from the building rained down like confetti from a parade celebration. People were running and trying to separate themselves from the smoke and falling debris.

"Since my office is located on the third floor and I was on crutches and really could not go anywhere at the time, I just waited for further direction from our building management staff. After a half-hour or so, we were told that all routes out of Manhattan were closed and that we should proceed on foot away from our building towards the Brooklyn Bridge. This was not a viable option for me, so remained inside my building. My sister-in-law also has an office in the building and I was able to find her in the company cafeteria. After about two hours, the smoke had cleared to the point that we could see reasonably well so we headed to the waterfront and were taken to New Jersey by tugboat.

"Since I have family and friends who worked in the World Trade Center, I was really concerned when I could not reach them initially upon arriving home. Thank God, all but one survived. My cousin, Shawn Powell, was one of the Brooklyn firemen that perished trying to save the lives of others.

"My concerns were for the many who were unable to get out of the building safely. I felt comforted that God still has a plan for my life that would not permit the enemy to interfere with that now. I give praise and thanks to my Lord and Savior, Jesus Christ, who has once again kept me out of harm's way. As I think back on the events of that day, I realize that my faith in God kept me from being fearful.

Timothy Davis

"My name is Timothy Davis and I worked in One World Trade Center on the 43rd Floor. On September 11, I was at my machine working when the first plane hit the tower I worked in. I felt the building shake and then heard the explosion. The next thing I did was run out into the hallway and to the cafeteria where I worked. I thought it was a gas leak, and that maybe something had happened there. When I reached the hallway, I looked up and the ceiling had fallen down, the lights were out, and water was all over the floor. I ran back to my office to tell my co-workers what I had seen. I told them it was bad and went through another entrance to the cafeteria to look out the window. I could see the debris and paper falling from the upper floors, and I came back and told the workers that it really looked bad. One of them said they thought we should go, so the next thing we did was get our things and leave.

"As we moved into the stairway, we saw that there were a lot of people already coming down from the upper floors. The stairwells were only wide enough for two people to fit side by side going down, and there was a long line of people already going down, trying to get out of the building. As we pressed our way out, we noticed some injured people coming down that we had to make way for. Their skin was peeling, and there were even some blind people trying to come down the stairs. We let one man go past who had a Seeing Eye™ dog. There were people who were on the stairway who were suffering from hysteria, so we let them pass as well.

"When we got down around the 23rd floor, we saw the fireman pressing their way upstairs to fight the fire. They were carrying hammers, large picks, and water hoses and had their oxygen tanks and masks on. It must have been very tiring and stressful, because they would have to stop on different floors to take a break and catch their breath because of the heavy equipment they were carrying upstairs. In those cases, we only had one lane going down because they would use the other lane to go up the stairs. We made a clear pathway for them to fight the fire as we also tried to go down out of the building.

"Someone had a cell phone and was trying to call to find out what was going on. That was the first time we heard that a plane had hit the building, but in my mind, I thought that maybe it was just a small plane. I still thought everything was all right. I would not find out the details until later.

"By the time we reached the ground floor, the entire floor was covered with water and we had to wade through to get out of the building. The water sprinklers were on from the ceiling above us so we were trying to press our way through the water to get to the open area.

"When we got outside, the medical team had a triage set up across the street in front of the Millennium Hotel, which was right across the street from the World Trade Center. They had doctors and ambulances, so we took the injured people we were trying to help there. I wanted to see what was going on so I looked up at the two building towers and noticed the flames jumping out from the building. As I was looking up to see what was going on, I saw the second tower start to fall. At that point, everyone turned and ran up Fulton Street towards Broadway. As we ran, people were falling in the street and other people were trying to jump over them. I ran out into the street and got halfway up the block when I started to get tired. I said, "God, give me strength so I can make it." When I got to the corner of Broadway and Fulton, I looked to my right down Broadway and saw a big cloud of smoke coming toward me. I turned left and started running in the opposite direction, but halfway down the block, I saw another cloud of smoke come around from the other direction towards me. The only thing I could think of to do was to run and grab a fence. Even as I ran over to the fence, I knew the cloud of smoke and debris would overtake me and was not sure what was in it or if the force would be enough to lift me off my feet and into the air. As it covered me, I felt the eerie feeling of death in the air and everything turned dark. The only thing that came to my mind was to say, 'Lord, save me!'

"I found that I had trouble breathing because of the debris. I had a rag in my hand, so I covered my nose and mouth with it and tried to breathe, but as I opened my mouth to breathe, I felt all the debris going into my mouth. I had a bottle of water and what came to my mind was to pour the water into the rag, which would cut down on the debris coming into my mouth. I poured the water into the rag and covered my nose and mouth and was able to breathe a little better. While I was standing there in the blackness just holding on, I could hear someone in the background saying, "Help me, help me!" The only thing I could say was, "Just stay where you are." The blackness was so great that you could not see anything. There was no help I could offer this person, and all I could say was, "Just stay right where you are. You'll be all right. Everything will be fine."

"In a few minutes, I felt something touch my back. I opened my eyes and all that darkness had dissipated a little and I was able to look into the dust floating through the air. At that point, you could see where to go. There was an officer standing in the street telling everyone to come into the restaurant. So, we ran into the restaurant to get out of the debris. We only stayed there for a few minutes. I left the building and walked down Broadway toward the Brooklyn Bridge. When I arrived, there were people covered with soot and debris, all trying to get over the wall to get into Brooklyn. I finally climbed over the wall and then started walking down Lafayette. The police were saying to walk north, and not to stop, as they did not know what else, if anything, might happen.

"As I walked down Lafayette, I saw One World Trade was still standing, so I thought that at least it had not fallen all the way down. When I got to Canal Street, I was trying to find a telephone to call someone to let them know I was alive and well, but there were too many people trying to make phone calls so I just kept walking. I got to 9th street, down to the Path station, and they said that no Path trains were running, so I came back out looking for a telephone to make contact. I realized that I did not have any change and decided to call my job collect. I could not get through, and suddenly realized that all the telephone lines in the office were tied into the World Trade Center, and it had collapsed. I called my church collect and they answered. I asked them to call my wife, pastor, and job and let them know that I was all right.

"When I arrived at Penn Station, everyone was standing outside. There were a lot of people waiting because authorities had made everyone leave the train station. They were standing in the street and we could see the ambulances and fire trucks racing downtown. People were walking, just trying to get out of the area. About 2:30 p.m., they started running trains back into New Jersey, so I was able to get a train to Newark. When I got to Newark, I was still covered in soot and debris. I talked to one of the gentlemen in the train station, and he said there was medical help outside. I went outside and the first thing they wanted to do was to hose me down. One of the doctors from University Hospital took my pulse and blood pressure and checked my breathing to make sure everything was all right. He said I seemed all right, but if I wanted to go to the hospital, they were waiting to get a group of people to put on a bus to the hospital for further examination. I told them that I felt all right and that I would rather go home to the hospital close to where I live. I left to go back inside to wait for the train and then saw a friend of mine who works for the Path Trains. He had a cell phone that he let me use to call some people. I contacted my wife to let her know that I was all right and then a train came, which I caught to Perth Amboy.

"When I arrived at Perth Amboy, I was able to go to the hospital where they took my blood pressure, pulse, and blood work and then gave me X-rays. After the X-rays and blood work came back, they gave me a prescription, and by the time I finished at the hospital, it was around 11:00 p.m. They said I was all right and that I did not seem to have swallowed anything. My sister-in-law, Carol Dortch-Wright, and her husband came to the hospital to pick me up and my other relatives came to see me.

"The next day, my sister-in-law called Bishop Hilliard and he called me at home. He spoke with me and I told him of my experience. He talked and prayed for me and said that if I needed any help, he and the church would be there for me."

Janet Bostic-Evans

"I am going to attempt to document how the tragic events of September 11, 2001 affected my life on that day and everyday since. Before I can do that, however, I need to talk a little about some of the history and events that lead up to that day.

"I am a political analyst and serve as the New Jersey Representative in the Government and Community Affairs Department at the Port Authority of New York and New Jersey. My primary responsibility is to establish and maintain working relationships with business, government, labor, and community leaders in New Jersey. I have worked at graduated levels of responsibility in the same department for almost 25 years. I worked in the North Tower, One World Trade Center for 24 years.

"It is amazing how much we take for granted. I had worked on the 68th floor of the World Trade Center for so long that I would routinely announce, "I'm home!" each and every morning as I entered my office. It was how I let my secretary and the rest of the staff know that I had arrived. I spent almost as much time there as I did in my own house, so it did feel like home. I had been working with the same people for so long that they did, indeed, feel like they were a part of my family.

"Back on February 26, 1993, when the bomb went off in the sub-level of the World Trade Center, along with most of my colleagues, I really believed that nothing could or would ever bring the building down. After all, it had survived a massive explosion that would have leveled most buildings and killed hundreds of people. The fatalities on February 26 were miraculously minimal. Port Authority staff and expertise had the building operating and open for business in just 6 weeks after the attack.

"Upon returning to the World Trade Center, the increased security measures were so tight after that first attack that even a 24-year veteran like myself could not get back into my office without an ID badge. There were days when I would forget to take it with me to lunch, or to run an errand on the WTC concourse. It was frustrating to be refused admittance by the same persons who looked into your eyes, smiled and greeted you every morning, noon and night as you entered and left the building. Yes, it was frustrating, yet comforting, at the same time. You just knew that you were going to be safe in that building.

· "I had so much of my life connected to the WTC over and above it being the place where I earned my income and living. I went to the WTC Dental Group. My pharmacist of 24 years was on the concourse of the WTC. My jeweler was there. I banked at the Credit Union in the WTC. I did most of my shopping there in New York. I even brought my children to work with me when they were out of school because they loved it so much. I had them with me in my office all day just 10 days before September 11. This is what I think about the most when I imagine how different the outcome of September 11 could have been if my children were there with me? Suppose it had happened while they were in the elevator on the way to the cafeteria? Suppose it had happened while they were on the 43rd floor and I was on the 68th floor? I never would have left that building without my children.

"On Friday, September 7, my secretary and I discussed the best way for her to better organize her personal papers, documents and receipts. I advised her to to start keeping her personal papers in order in one of the cabinets right there at her desk. I proudly unlocked the files containing everything from my life, car, and homeowners insurance policies to the deed on my house. "After all," I said to her, "it cannot be any more convenient or safer than it is right here in the World

Trade Center. This is where we spend most of our time and where we conduct most of our necessary personal business, too." She agreed with me, and vowed to start bringing in her important papers next week.

"On Sunday, September 9, my back started to bother me and even though I believed that it was psychosomatic, I decided that I was not going to go into New York the next day and possibly the entire week.

"On Monday, September 10, I could not tell whether it was psychosomatic or not, but my back really did hurt and all I wanted to do was to lie down. I did not get much rest because my boss and secretary called me several times throughout the day to talk about a new crisis. I was also told that there was a meeting scheduled at the last minute to discuss a project of mine on Tuesday, September 11 at 1:00 p.m. in the Port Department, so I rose to the occasion and agreed to attend. I made up my mind to go into my New York office earlier than usual to familiarize myself with the possible subject matter of the upcoming meeting. However, just before 5:00 p.m., I received another call from my secretary telling me that before I came into New York, I needed to go to an Urban League Board meeting in Newark.

"September 11 was a sunny day, and I love sunny days. I feel better when the sun shines, so I thanked God for making it easier for me to leave the house and abandon my plans to rest for the remainder of the week. I got the girls off to school and enjoyed a leisurely morning getting ready to be in Newark by 9:30 a.m. While putting on a little make-up in my bathroom, I heard that my regular news show had been interrupted for a special report, so I left the bathroom and stood in front of the television. I was aghast when I saw the picture of my office building apparently on fire with black smoke coming out of the top half of the building. I immediately dialed the main information number in Media Relations to ask them what was going on. Bob answered the phone and sounded calm. I told him what I saw on T.V. and asked if he needed any help. He thanked me and told me that Media Relations had the press calls under control. I hung up and immediately called my own office. Beverly, the departmental secretary, was still there answering the phone. I told her that it looked bad, asked who was there with her, and advised her to leave. She said that her boss had just left, but that he was coming back and she did not know if she should leave. I told her again, "Get out of the building, now!"

"After we hung up, I called Bob again, who was still answering the phones and asked him if he wanted me to come over. When he said that they were about to leave the building, I hung up and re-dialed Beverly. Much to my surprise and disappointment, she answered the phone again. I could hear that she was frightened, confused, and alone. Her boss never returned. I told her in as calm and serious a voice as I could to get her things and get out of there.

"As soon as I hung up the phone, it rang. It was a good friend and colleague. She was crying and screaming that she was "never going to go back into the World Trade Center." Neither of us knew at the time how true that statement was about to become. She had just missed being in the World Trade Center when the first attack took place in February 1993. We cried and prayed together for a while, and then I told her that I needed to call my parents to let them know that I was okay.

"As soon as I put down the phone, it rang again. This time it was my ex-husband, AJ. The relief that I heard in his voice surprised me, and I was secretly grateful for his concern. As I hung up the phone, I looked at the television to see another plane flying directly into the second tower. It appeared to have flown into the building at the same level on which my office was located in One WTC. I could not process what I was seeing. I knew that it was real, but I just could not believe it.

"There was no more doubt about what had happened. It was deliberate! The World Trade Center—my house—had been deliberately attacked and was burning out of control! All I could think was, "This is it! The world is coming to an end! This is the beginning of Armageddon…World War III! The phone rang and it was AJ again. "Go and get the girls from school now!" he nearly commanded. "I am on my way home. I will see you in a little while." Before leaving to pick up my children, I dialed my office, again. There was no answer this time.

"By the time I got back from picking up my daughters, 2 WTC already had collapsed. When I opened the door for AJ a short time later, we both started crying at the sight of each other. He reached out with one arm to embrace the girls who were behind me, and we all cried together for a while.

"For some reason, I kept calling my office, but by this time the lines were completely dead and did not even ring. Then I tried to call my secretary, Pam, at home and left her a message to call me as soon as she got back. Her daughter called me later from college in Maryland to let me know that Pam was okay, but unable to get through to me.

"That night, I called as many of my colleagues as I could to check on them. Everyone had been accounted for except Beverly, the departmental secretary. I called her home, but there was no answer other than her service. The next day, my manager decided that she would go into the command center that had been set up in Jersey City to see if there was anything that she could do to help. She promised to call and let me know what was going on. I told her that I was going to my church where my pastor was holding a special prayer service for the victims and the missing. I wanted to thank God for His divine mercy and intervention at having spared my life once again, and I wanted to pray for Beverly, who was still missing and who was the single parent of a 13-year-old girl.

"I know that Bishop Hilliard is only a man, but I honestly believe that he is a man who has been anointed by God to do His work here on earth. The Lord is still working on me. I do not go to church every Sunday, and I still do a lot of things that I know that I should not, but since I started going to Second Baptist under the guidance and tutelage of Bishop Hilliard, I have become a better person. That he would even think to hold a special service for those of us who had been personally touched by this tragedy was incredible to me.

"The service was wonderful! You would have had to

have been an emotional zombie not to feel the Spirit of the Holy Ghost moving throughout the church on that day. The Bishop asked that we say the names of those lost and missing out loud and pray for their safety and their souls. I tearfully prayed for Beverly throughout the entire service and felt guilty for not being there with her. At the same time, I was grateful that I was alive and still able to see and hold my children, and I knew that God understood what I was feeling even when I did not understand it myself. As usual, God had spoken to us through Bishop Hilliard, and I left church feeling so much better than I had felt before I arrived.

"When I came home, there was a message from Beverly thanking me for my concern. She said that she had been buried in the falling debris of Tower One, but that the force had thrown her against a wall where there was an air pocket. She said that she had been unable to speak but could only hold up her arm. She also described how scared she had been to feel how close the beams of steel and concrete had fallen near her, obviously burying the people who had been only steps behind her just moments before, yet sparing her. She had not been able to call anyone because she was hospitalized, and there were no working phone lines.

A few days later, I spoke to Beverly personally, and she described what it was like to have been inside the building as it burned and collapsed. She could not get over the fact that her boss, for whom she had worked for the previous six years, had left her there and never called back to tell her to leave. She said that she and a co-worker had stayed behind to help Tina, a woman who was confined to a wheelchair. Tina's manager and colleagues also had left the floor without helping her. They secured Tina in a portable wheelchair and left the 68th floor. They encountered a young man who took Tina down the stairs. The story was later featured on Date Line, Oprah, Rosie O'Donnell and numerous other talk shows, but there was never any mention made of the women who were really responsible for saving Tina's life.

At the end of our telephone conversation, Beverly thanked me for calling her so many times. She said that she was so scared yet so trusting of her boss that she would have stayed there to wait for him if I had not called so many times and told her to leave. She stopped short of thanking me for saving her life. Since she is a Christian, she knew who was really responsible for saving our lives that day.

He that dwelleth in the secret place
of the Most High shall abide under the
shadow of the Almighty. I will say of the
Lord, He is my refuge and my fortress:
my God, in Him will I trust.
Psalm 91:1-2

Rudy Bacchus
(1953 – 2001)

"Jesus said…I am the resurrection, and the life:
he that believeth in me, though he were dead,
yet shall he live" (John 11:25).

Very few among us have escaped witnessing some kind of tragedy. While we have seen bad things happen, it never really affects us significantly until it happens to someone that we know and love. I mentioned that I memorialized two members of our church that were lost in the attacks on September 11. I would like to share with you the life of one of those members who was lost in the attacks on the World Trade Center.

Tragedy does have a face. For our congregation, the faces included those of Rudy Bacchus and Perry Thompson. Rudy's story is both tragic and triumphant.

Eustace Patrick Rudyard Bacchus, or "Rudy," as he preferred to be addressed, came to America from the Republic of Guyana, South America. Rudy always seemed to know exactly what he wanted, where he wanted to go, and how to get there. None of this, however, ever distracted him from enjoying life. He loved to dance and took particular pride in his ability to perform on the dance floor to the strains of 'Kung Fu Fighting,' or to what he thought was an excellent Fox Trot, Mambo, or Waltz. Other than his family, he loved the camera best, not standing before it, but behind it. His love of photography probably led to his addiction with gadgets. Rudy loved gadgets as much for what they did to improve his daily life and enhance his utilization of time as he did for exploring their inner workings. He loved to know what made them tick and why. His latest hand-held computer was his pride and joy.

In 1971, Rudy enrolled at Brooklyn College where he earned an accounting degree. Because he did not want to be just a bean counter, he chose to seek his fortune on Wall Street where he had obtained part-time work during his college years. He joined Merrill Lynch & Company in 1975 as a clerk in the Wire and Order Department. He threw himself into his work and in February of 1982, he met his soul mate Juana Maria Coley of the Canal Zone, Panama. Rumor has it that he proposed at the time of their first meeting. However, for Rudy, it was an agonizing three months until Juana accepted his proposal. They were married in1982 by the Honorable David Dinkins, Clerk of the City of New York, and united in Christian marriage in 1983 at the Lutheran church of the Prince of Peace, Cambria Heights, New York.

The union of Rudy and Juana was truly blessed with the birth of Carla Nicole in 1984, to join Humberto, Juana's son by her previous marriage. In 1995, Rudy was appointed an Assistant Vice President of Merrill Lynch & Company. In that same year, the Reverend Larry Williams ordained him a Deacon of the Second Baptist Church of Metuchen, New Jersey. In 1996, he was appointed Vice President of Merrill Lynch & Company, a position he held until he went into business for himself as an independent stockbroker.

By the time of his transition from this life to the next at the World Trade Center Towers, he was in business for himself and, "being Rudy," was fully engaged in it. He had also moved on to and became a member of our church—the Cathedral-Second Baptist Church of Perth Amboy—and was getting himself fully engaged there as well. Rudy was a committed husband and father, an honorable son and brother, a faithful Christian, and a dedicated member of our church.

Rudy was at the World Trade Center at the top of the towers having a breakfast meeting when the planes hit. The Sunday before the 11th, I preached on preparing for the future. I dealt with preparing for death (i.e., having insurance, making sure that you have a will and that your affairs are in order). I also talked about how important it is for us to honor God with our livelihood. I emphasized the responsibility that we have to those who come after us, and how we do not want to leave our children and our loved ones destitute. Juana told me later that at that very moment, Rudy nudged her and they looked at each other because he had everything in order. He was a prepared man. And I do not mean just prepared because he had a will, an estate plan, stocks, and insurance. I do not mean he was a prepared man because he had a home and cars. He was prepared in his soul and his spirit. When he nudged Juana on that morning in September, he was celebrating the fact that he was in order and that he was prepared.

On the 11th of September, in the split second when the plane hit the World Trade Center, he never felt it. In a moment, in the twinkling of an eye, he saw a light brighter than he had ever seen before. Rudy transitioned from this life to life eternal. The devil, Satan, evil, wickedness, and terrorism got no victory there.

Our hearts went out to Rudy's family. We love them deeply and were all moved and deeply affected by his death. Our hearts were torn. Although we came together to celebrate Rudy's life, underneath all of the celebration, there was weariness. We were weary of the news...weary of watching the collapse of the World Trade Center towers over and over and over again.

The following is a famous poem that was often quoted by Dr. Benjamin Elijah Maze of Morehouse College...

We only have one minute, only sixty seconds in
it. We did not seek it, we did not choose it.
Thrust upon us, we can't refuse it. But we will all
suffer, all of us will suffer if we lose it. And give
an account if we abuse it. One tiny little minute,
but eternity is in it.

With the minute that God has given us, what are we
doing with our lives? Whom have we helped and loved,
and who will mourn for us and speak well of us? Who
will say of us when we leave here, "You know my life is
changed because this person passed this way. My life has
changed because she prayed for me. My life has changed
because they made it happen. My life has changed because they took the time to help me."

What are we doing with the minute that each of us
has? The 11th of September made us all think of our
own mortality. In one moment, all of our wealth and all
of the symbols of national security can crumble. What,
indeed, does it profit a man, a woman, a boy, or girl, to
gain the whole world and lose their soul? I am glad that
Rudy's soul was right with God, and that he is with Him
now.

We came together on the day of Rudy's funeral, not
to focus on the evil inflicted on him, but to celebrate the
life of Rudy Bacchus and countless others. This man
knew what it was to work hard. He also worked for God
who had done so much in his life. When he came to our
church, Rudy did not serve as a deacon, but his wife and
daughter did work in the church. In fact, the Sunday before the 11th, Juana read the Scripture in Spanish at the

8:30 a.m. service. They were faithful worshipers and church workers while coming to our church. Juana found her niche in the Spanish speaking ministry, while Rudy chose to be still and grow in the Lord. Having served in his former church, he had served and given so much. By the time he came to our church, he felt a need to sit and be fed, to worship and grow. He was faithful in his worship, faithful in his giving, and faithful in his commitment. The media ministry team told me that he was faithful at the Tape Table, always purchasing tapes, ministering, and sharing ministry with others.

How should we remember Rudy and others like him? Once they are gone from us, how can we respect their memories? Rather than giving in to wickedness, we must continue to testify that light overcomes the darkness and ultimately right overcomes wrong.

We honor their memories by continuing the good works they have begun. In the book of Revelation, the Apostle John declares,

> Then I heard a voice from heaven say, "Write: Blessed are the dead who die in the Lord from now on" "Yes," says the Spirit, "they will rest from their labour, for their deeds will follow them" (Rev. 14:13).

We should focus, not on what evil has done to Rudy, but on who Rudy was. We cannot talk about who this man was without talking about the God who loved him and the God who kept him. We cannot remember him without thinking about the God who directed, covered, prospered, and empowered him, and opened up his heart. God touched the heart of this dedicated member, friend of pastors, faithful and loving father and husband, caring son, and devoted brother.

Over the weeks following Rudy's death, I observed Juana carefully. She has, by the grace of God, weathered the storm. She has not missed one worship service since September 11, 2001. She has been in church every Sunday and every Thursday, giving God the praise, the glory, and the honor that He deserves. This is Rudy's legacy.

The Scriptures say that love never dies. The body dies, but many of us can still feel the love of parents or children who have died many years ago. Love never dies. There will come a day when the wicked will cease from troubling the righteous, and the weary soul shall be at rest.

The Bible teaches that heaven is an eternal place. I am not worried about where it is, as long as I know it is going to be where Jesus is. Christians do not have to walk around with their shoulders bent, feeling discouraged and despondent. Think of it. We can have the joy, peace, and forgiveness that He offers us and then heaven, too. We can take comfort in knowing that the Lord will be there, and that Rudy is there, too.

To the memory of my beloved father, Rudy Bacchus:

Father and I Lost

Father of mine, where have you gone? My days run so long without you being by my side. Every day turns a little bit colder. Every day I see my mother weak with tear-filled eyes, and I cannot seem to understand her reasons. I still feel you near to my heart, my soul, though everyone says you are gone.

Father, why have you abandoned me? I am so lost without you. I cannot seem to grasp the right touch or smell of you. I cannot seem to find the right words of wisdom, I feel so alone. I am trying to find you in my dreams, though every hand I grab is not yours. The bright light of souls blinds me. I would rather walk with you in the dark than walk alone in the light, though you are nowhere to be found.

Every day I am trying to find you...every minute I am thinking of you...every hour I am alone.

I miss you Daddy,
Love, Carla Nicole

To contact the author, write or call

Millennium Ministries
The Cathedral Second Baptist Church
P.O. Box 1608
Perth Amboy, New Jersey 08862
1-800-YES-LORD
website: www.thecathedral.org

*Please note that a portion of the proceeds
from the sale of this book will be donated
toward those affected by 9-11.*

OTHER BOOKS BY DONALD HILLIARD, JR.

SAFE HARBOR BEGINS @HOME
How to develop effective parenting skills that empower
you to build a safe and secure family.
ISBN 1-58169-069-X PB 96 pg.

SOMEBODY SAY YES!
Answers to the most pressing issues of the new millennium. Is success within our reach—are we ready for it? Is
holiness within our hearts—can we embrace it? Is the
family within our priorities—will we nurture it?
ISBN 1-58169-062-2 hardcover 160 pg.

STOP THE FUNERAL!
This book defines the problems facing today's young
people in a hard-hitting, no-holds-barred fashion.
ISBN 1-57778-116-3 PB 212 pg.